okinawa 1945

the last battle

GORDON ROTTMAN

okinawa 1945

the last battle

Praeger Illustrated Military History Series

PRAEGER

Westport, Connecticut
London

Library of Congress Cataloging-in-Publication Data

Rottman, Gordon L.
    Okinawa 1945 : the last battle / Gordon L. Rottman.
       p. cm – (Praeger illustrated military history, ISSN 1547-206X)
    Originally published: Oxford: Osprey, 2002.
    Includes bibliographical references and index.
    ISBN 0-275-98274-2 (alk. paper)
    1. World War, 1939–1945 – Campaigns – Japan – Okinawa Island. I. Title. II. Series.
    D767.99.O45R68   2004
    940.54'252294–dc22 2003064189

British Library Cataloguing in Publication Data is available.

Library of Congress Catalog Card Number: 2003064189
ISBN: 0-275-98274-2
ISSN: 1547-206X

Praeger Publishers, 88 Post Road West, Westport, CT 06881
An imprint of Greenwood Publishing Group, Inc.
www.praeger.com

Printed in China through World Print Ltd.

The paper used in this book complies with the Permanent Paper Standard issued
by the National Information Standards Organization (Z39.48-1984).

10 9 8 7 6 5 4 3 2 1

ILLUSTRATED BY: Howard Gerrard

CONTENTS

KEY TO MILITARY SYMBOLS

XXXXX ARMY GROUP	XXXX ARMY	XXX CORPS	XX DIVISION	X BRIGADE
III REGIMENT	II BATTALION	I COMPANY	INFANTRY	CAVALRY
ARTILLERY	ARMOUR	MOTORIZED	AIRBORNE	SPECIAL FORCES

STRATEGIC SITUATION, MARCH 1945

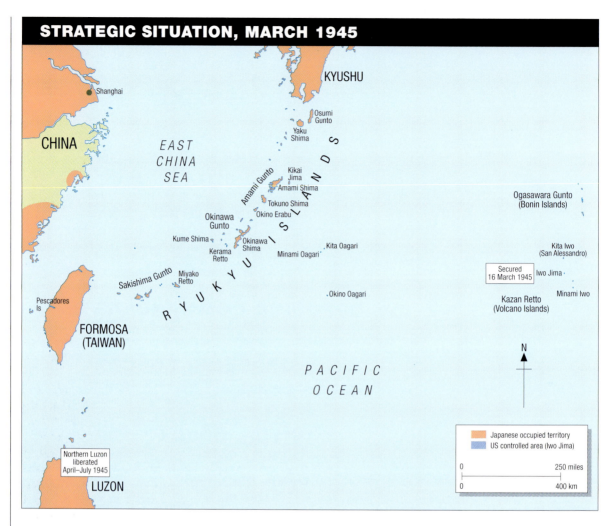

KYUSHU

Shanghai

CHINA

EAST
CHINA
SEA

Osumi
Gunto

Yaku
Shima

Kikai
Jima

Amami Gunto

Amami Shima

Tokuno Shima

Okino Erabu

Okinawa
Gunto

Kume Shima

Okinawa
Shima

Kerama
Retto

Minami Oagari

Kita Oagari

Ogasawara Gunto
(Bonin Islands)

R Y U K Y U   I S L A N D S

Sakishima Gunto

Miyako
Retto

Pescadores
Is

FORMOSA
(TAIWAN)

Kita Iwo
(San Alessandro)

Secured
16 March 1945

Iwo Jima

Minami Iwo

Kazan Retto
(Volcano Islands)

Okino Oagari

N

PACIFIC
OCEAN

| | Japanese occupied territory |
| | US controlled area (Iwo Jima) |

0   250 miles

0   400 km

Northern Luzon
liberated
April–July 1945

LUZON

INTRODUCTION

The spring of 1945 found Allied fortunes in the Pacific very much in the ascendant. A series of victorious campaigns had reclaimed many of the islands and territories seized by the Imperial Japanese forces at the end of 1941 and the early months of 1942. The dark days of humiliating defeats were long behind the unstoppable Allied juggernaut. There was no doubt who would be the ultimate victor. The only questions remaining were when the final battle would be fought and how many more men would have to die to set right a grievous wrong.

Allied strategy entailed three thrusts across the Pacific. In the North Pacific Area the US Army and Navy, backed by Canadians, cleared the Japanese from Alaska's Aleutian Islands. In the Southwest Pacific Area, General Douglas MacArthur had at his disposal combined US Army, US Marine, Australian, and New Zealand forces with the Third and Seventh Fleets mainly supported by land-based aircraft. They first secured the line of communications between the US and Australia. Then they seized the Solomon Islands, with the main objective being Rabaul on New Britain, and thrust along New Guinea's north coast aiming at the Philippines.

In the Central Pacific Area the Fifth Fleet, supported by carrier-based aircraft, secured the Gilberts in late 1943, with the ultimate objective being the Japanese base at Truk Atoll in the Carolines. The Japanese bastions at Rabaul and Truk were neutralized by air power and bypassed. The Fifth Fleet went on to seize the Marshalls in early 1944. The Fifth and Third Fleets' next target was the Mariana Islands. The seizure of the Marianas proved to be an extremely serious blow to Japan. Part of the Mandated Territories bequeathed to Japan by the League of Nations in 1919, the former German possessions were considered part of the Japanese Empire. The fall of Saipan and neighboring Tinian in July 1944, followed by the liberation of Guam in August, led to such an outcry in Japan that General Shigenori Tojo was forced to resign as prime minister and a new cabinet was formed.

MacArthur invaded Leyte in the Philippines in October 1944 with the Sixth Army and Seventh Fleet. By the end of the year they had secured several solid footholds in the massive archipelago. The Philippines was finally declared liberated on 5 July 1945, two weeks after Okinawa was secured. In the meantime the Third Fleet took Iwo Jima between February and March 1945.

The Japanese knew what was coming next. What they did not know was exactly where the Americans would strike. The Imperial General Headquarters (IGHQ) narrowed the possible targets to Formosa off the Chinese mainland or Okinawa southwest of the Home Islands. The Japanese began to reinforce both areas as the American Fifth Fleet and Tenth Army marshaled at island bases across the Pacific.

LEFT **An aerial view of Okinawa Shima looking north. The island's southern tip, Cape Kiyan, is cut off, but most of the south of the island, where the battle was largely fought out, is shown. (US Army)**

A photograph of the Katchin Hanto (Peninsula) area on the east coast taken on 2 June 1945 shows the open areas encountered on much of southern Okinawa. (US Army)

PLANNING *ICEBERG*

The battle for Okinawa is said by some to have begun in May 1944; a year before the landing. During the lull before the Marianas landings, Admiral Earnest J. King, Chief of Naval Operations and Commander-in-Chief, US Fleet, met with Admirals Chester W. Nimitz, Commander-in-Chief, Pacific Fleet/Commander, Pacific Ocean Area (CinCPAC/POA), and William F. Halsey, Commander, Third Fleet, in San Francisco to discuss future Pacific Theater strategy. A major concern was the possibility that Japan might conclude a separate peace with a hard-pressed China. Nimitz suggested establishing US positions on the coast of China and opening supply lines to the interior. Supplying the massive, but ill-equipped, Chinese Army would force Japan to reinforce the mainland and stretch its forces. Consideration was given to invading Formosa, 670 miles (1,079 km) southwest of Japan, before it could be reinforced, and thereby bypass the Philippines.

Formosa, basically a Japanese colony, had its advantages. Bypassing the Philippines would prevent a potentially protracted campaign requiring a massive commitment of US forces. Formosa would provide a base from which to invade the mainland, protect sea routes to China, and launch long-range bombers at Japan. B-29 Superfortresses of the Twentieth Air Force were operating out of southern China at extreme range and experiencing major difficulties receiving supplies and fuel from India.

Formosa could be a problem as well, however. It was well within range of Japanese air bases on mainland China, was garrisoned by substantial forces[1], could be easily reinforced from the mainland only

100 miles (161 km) away, and was a large mountainous land mass 240 miles (386 km) long and 90 miles (145 km) wide, with elevations to 13,000 ft (3,943 m). It promised to be a tough campaign; Formosa was about the size of Kyushu, the southernmost island of Japan.

In July 1944, with the Marianas campaign winding up, President Roosevelt met with Admiral Nimitz and General MacArthur. Nimitz, as Commander, Pacific Ocean Area, controlled the South, Central, and North Pacific Areas from his headquarters at Pearl Harbor. MacArthur commanded forces coming out of Australia in the Southwest Pacific and New Guinea[2]. He opposed the plan to bypass the Philippines contending that, with additional naval support, he had the forces to liberate them. Nimitz agreed to an alternate plan that included recapturing much of the Philippines between October and December 1944. Depending on the situation, either Luzon would be invaded in February 1945 or Formosa–Amoy Area (on mainland China) in March. This would be followed by the Bonins (Chichi Jima) in April and the Ryukyus (with Okinawa) in May. MacArthur insisted on liberating Manila on Luzon, determined to fulfil the promise he made to return on his departure in March 1942.

Soon after the proposed plan was developed, Lieutenant-General Millard F. Harmon, Army Air Forces, Pacific Ocean Area, proposed that Operation *Causeway* – Formosa – be abandoned with compelling arguments that air operations could more effectively be conducted against Japan from the Marianas. He pointed out the threat posed by remaining hostile forces (it was not to be completely occupied because

This aerial photograph of the Motobu Peninsula on Okinawa's upper west coast where the 6th Mar. Div. fought, demonstrates the ruggedness of Okinawa's terrain. Sesoko Shima can be seen in the background; this is a comparatively small area when viewed in the context of the entire 640 sq mile (1,658 sq km) island and provides an idea as to the island's magnitude. (USMC)

A typical Okinawan rural village with thatch-roofed houses surrounded by mud or stone walls. Windbreaks of hedges and large bushes grow along the walls. Camouflaged Japanese trucks can be seen at the top of the photograph. (US Army)

of its size), possible interception from the Chinese mainland along the entire route to Japan, and less favorable weather. Harmon proposed that Iwo Jima in the Volcano Islands (south of Japan) be seized in January 1945 and Okinawa (southwest of Japan) in June, simultaneous with the invasion of Luzon. General Robert C. Richardson, US Army Forces, Pacific Ocean Area, agreed with Harmon. Other key commanders tagged for *Causeway* favored the proposal. General Simon B. Buckner, Tenth Army, stated sufficient combat and service troops were not available to secure a significant lodgment on Formosa. Admiral Raymond A. Spruance also preferred to avoid Formosa.

In October 1944, Nimitz advised Admiral King of his subordinate commanders' views. The Joint Chiefs of Staff evaluated the proposals and directed MacArthur to land on Luzon on 20 December 1944, and Nimitz to assault Iwo Jima on 20 January 1945 and Okinawa on 1 March. This last operation before the November invasion of Japan was code-named *Iceberg*. The Ryukyu Islands Group was codenamed *Bunkhouse* and Okinawa itself was designated *Scattering*.

A ridge-side gorge in the Awacha Pocket viewed from Wilson Ridge in May. This area, 2,000 yds (1,829 m) north of Shuri, was a maze of gorges and steep hills. Such gorges were honeycombed with dugouts and fighting positions covering the approaches and both sides. A force attacking one side was fired on from the other as well as from above. It took the 5th Marines, 1st Mar. Div. from 3–11 May to seize the pocket held by elements of the Japanese 62nd Division. (USMC)

With the US fully securing the Philippines, Japanese forces in the Dutch East Indies would be cut off from the Home Islands. B-29s could ceaselessly bomb Japan from their bases in the Marianas with the Japanese denied bases in the Ryukyus from which to intercept them. American bases in the Ryukyus would further protect the flank by intercepting enemy aircraft from Formosa and China, and they could attack Japan as well. Seizing Iwo Jima, midway between the Marianas and Japan, would allow fighters to rendezvous with and escort the bombers, and provide stricken B-29s with emergency airfields. The forces and command structure devised for Formosa would be retained for the invasion of Okinawa Gunto. In the meantime, the Third Fleet and III Amphibious Corps assaulted the Palau Islands in September 1944 to secure MacArthur's eastern flank while he conducted initial operations in the Philippines[3]. The Fifth Fleet and V Amphibious Corps assaulted the critical target of Iwo Jima on 19 February 1945, over a month and a half late due to operational necessity, in a vicious battle presaging future events on Okinawa. It would not be secured by V Corps' three Marine divisions until 16 March. Within days the initial operations for *Iceberg* began, delayed by the hold-ups in the Iwo Jima operation.

RYUKYU ISLANDS

The Nansei Shoto (Southwestern Islands) is a curving string of widely spaced islands stretching southwest from Kyushu, the southernmost of the Japanese Home Islands, across the East China Sea to Formosa. Ryukyu Retto comprises most islands in the Nansei Shoto string. The Ryukyus consists of 161 islands in five major groups: Osumi, Torkara, Amami, Okinawa, and Sakishima Guntos. Okinawa is the centerpiece and largest jewel of the Ryukyus[4].

Okinawa Gunto includes several islands and groups satellited around the main island: Kerama Retto (eight islands 15 miles/24 km west of Okinawa), Kume Shima (55 miles/89 km west), Agunia Shima (40 miles/64 km west), Ie Shima (4 miles/6.5 km west), Iheya Retto (four islands 15 miles/24 km north), Yoron Shima (15 miles/24 km northeast), and an unnamed group of eight scattered islands called the Eastern Islands by the Americans (5–10 miles/8–16 km east). Most of these islands would play important roles in the Okinawa campaign.

Okinawa Gunto is approximately 320 miles (515 km) southwest of Kyushu. It lies 350 miles (564 km) northeast of Formosa and 450 miles (725 km) east of the Chinese mainland. It is in time zone 21, the same as Japan, what the US called time zone *Item* or *Zulu-9*, *Zulu* being Greenwich meantime.

The Chinese intermittently raided the Ryukyus for hundreds of years beginning in the 6th or 7th century. The Dragon Empire never attempted to attain complete sovereignty over the islands, but in 1368 demanded tribute and the Ryukyuan king declared himself a subject of China. Okinawa also had relations with Japan but managed to remain at least partly independent of both its dominating imperial neighbors. Japan gained partial control of the islands in the 1500s. In 1609, after Okinawa refused to provide troops for Japan's war against Korea, Japan invaded and devastated the island kingdom. Okinawa still maintained a semi-independent status, paying tribute to both Japan and China. Commodore Matthew Perry used Okinawa as a supply base during his 1853 effort to establish trade with Japan. He raised an American flag on a hill near Shuri Castle that Americans would die for almost 100 years later. The opening up of Japan quickly established the country as a regional power, and it took control of Okinawa in 1867. The Okinawan king was given a permanent residence in Tokyo and in 1874 the Japanese Home Ministry took total control of the islands. A Japanese governor was installed in 1879 and the islands given prefecture *(ken)* status. China still claimed the islands and Okinawans preferred their fence-sitting status between the two powers, but they were now solidly part of the Empire of the Rising Sun. Okinawa was granted a prefecture assembly and a seat in the Diet in 1920. In 1943, the Prefecture of Okinawa was consolidated with seven others into the Home Islands District of Kyushu.

Okinawa Shima is oriented northeast to southwest with a length of 64 miles (100 km). Its width varies from 18 miles (29 km) at the Motobu Peninsula *(hanto)* extending east from the island's northern portion to 2 miles (3.2 km) at the Ishikawa Isthmus just south of the island's mid-point. Several smaller peninsulas extend from the island's southern portion protecting excellent anchorages. The Ishikawa Isthmus divides Okinawa into two contrasting regions.

The sparsely populated north is covered with rugged, ridge-like 1,000–1,500-ft (300–450 m) high hills branching off a central ridge. The areas around the hills are bisected by deep ravines and gullies terminating at the coast in steep cliffs. The northwest coast's Motobu Peninsula is a dominant feature and was the center of Japanese resistance in the north. The entire area is covered by dense forests of pine, live oak, and thick underbrush. The road system was extremely limited, with only one single-track road following the northwest shore to

The Japanese used every available natural terrain and manmade feature for defensive purposes. These concrete-lined rainwater catchment basins, linked to the rice paddy irrigation system, were used as fighting positions. Here marines examine an Arisaka rifle. (USMC)

the north end. Cross-country vehicle movement was impossible. The soil is red clay and sandy loam and is well drained by the many small streams. This difficult terrain stretches south past the Ishikawa Isthmus to the island's southern one-third.

The heavily populated south is characterized by rolling hills, sometimes terraced, gradually climbing to over 500 ft (152 m) high at the island's southern end. The hills are cut by ravines and shallow, narrow streams that provide poor drainage. Caves *(gama)*, cut by underground streams, honeycomb the hills and ridges. The further south one goes, the more hilly and broken the terrain becomes. The central plains south of the Ishikawa Isthmus are open and gently rolling. Further south, small scattered, irregular knolls dot the area, and these were incorporated into the Japanese defenses. The hills can be steep in some areas and several escarpments and twisting limestone ridges cut across the island providing successive cross-compartment defensive lines as one advances south. There were few long fields of fire, so conditions were ideal for Japanese short-range weapons. While some areas were lightly wooded, four-fifths of the south was cultivated with sweet potato, sugar cane, rice, and soybean fields in the valleys and on hills and plateaus. Although secondary to farming, fishing was also one of the island's principal industries. Villages and towns were scattered across the southern region and connected by a network of single-track roads and trails; some of which were surfaced with crushed coral, but most were dirt cart tracks. A single two-lane limestone road connected the island's only two cities of Naha and Shuri. Because of the clay soil conditions, the largely unimproved roads were totally incapable of supporting military traffic during the rainy season. Off-road traffic was impossible in most areas when the rains came. A narrow-gauge (60-cm) railroad connected Naha,

An aerial view of the north end of Tokashiki Shima looking south. This is the largest island in the Kerama Retto. The islands unsuccessfully served the Japanese as a suicide boat base and the US as a fleet base. The small bay on the upper right coast is one of the 27 March US landing beaches. (US Army)

Kobakura, Kobuba, and Yonabaru with branches linking Kobakura to Kadena and Kokuba with Itoman. The 30 miles (48 km) of track mainly hauled produce, and some of it would be returned to operation by American engineers.

Much of the coastline was fronted by limestone cliffs and scattered coral heads. The most desirable landing beaches were on the west coast, south of the two-mile (3.2-km) wide Ishikawa Isthmus, the Hagushi Beaches[5] edging the central plains. The usual coral-reef shelf paralleled the shore with a higher seaward crest 200–700 yds (183–640 m) offshore that deepened closer to shore. At low tide, trucks could easily drive across it. The area's mean tides are 4 ft 1 in. (1.24 m), but at the time of the landing a spring tide would raise the water level to 5 ft 11 in. (1.79 m). The eight miles (13 km) of landing beaches were gently sloping with few natural obstacles, although there were extensive sea walls 3–10 ft (0.9–3 m) high. The beaches were not continuous, but separated into lengths between 100 and 900 yds (90–820 m) long by low-cliff headlands. At low tide the beaches were 10–45 yds (9–41 m) wide, but at high water were completely awash. Behind the beaches sparsely vegetated and cultivated ground rose gradually to 50 ft (15 m). The beaches were selected because of their proximity to Yontan and Kadena airfields 2,000 yds (1,820 m) inland. Their early seizure would allow land-based fighters to fly close air support and aid in the defense of the fleet.

The population of Okinawa was 435,000 and included thousands of Japanese immigrants serving as government officials, administrators, managers, and merchants. Even with representation in the government, Okinawans had little real say in their affairs. Naha is Okinawa's prefectural capital and commercial center with a pre-invasion population of over 60,000. It was the island's main seaport. Shuri was slightly smaller and was the Ryukyu's traditional capital. Shuri Castle is perched on the massive

ABOVE **A marine intelligence team examine a weapon first encountered on Iwo Jima, the 320-mm spigot mortar. The black-painted projectile with a thin red band, weighed 675 lb and had a range of barely 1,000 yds. Manned by the Japanese 1st Independent Mortar Regiment, its 24 mortars were inaccurate and proved to be none too effective despite their massive warhead. (USMC)**

ABOVE, RIGHT **The embrasure of a concrete and limestone 10.5-cm Model 14 (1925) gun emplacement dug into the side of a hill. While provided with a limited field of fire, it and other widely dispersed guns were able to concentrate their fires on specific areas through which it was predicted the enemy would advance. Similar positions were constructed of logs rather than concrete. They were also built for 15-cm Model 89 (1929) guns and Model 96 (1936) howitzers. Small in size, the embrasures were difficult to detect from the air and hard to knockout from the ground as they required multiple direct hits. The gun could be pulled well back into the tunnel when fire was directed at the embrasure. The scattered logs had probably been stacked in front as camouflage. (USMC)**

ridge cutting across the island and was the ancient throne of the Ryukyuan kings. It would become a vicious battleground.

Most population centers were villages ranging from fewer than 100 inhabitants to over 1,000. The towns of Itoman, Nago, and Yonabaru were simply large villages with few modern buildings. Concrete and stone government and commercial buildings were numerous in Naha and Shuri, but most urban buildings and dwellings were one-storey wood, surrounded by low stone walls. Dwellings in villages had clay walls, thatch roofs, and were surrounded by bamboo windbreaks or low stone or mud walls overgrown with tropical vegetation. Unique to Okinawa were the stone, lyre-shaped family tombs, which were an important part of the indigenous animistic cult, emphasizing the veneration of ancestors. Dug into hillsides, they did not offer all-around defense, but provided protection from artillery and their vulnerable sides could be covered from other fighting positions.

The two main airfields, Yontan and Kadena (also known as Yara Hikojo), were on the central plains while Machinato Airfield was just north of Naha. Across from it on the east coast was abandoned Yonabaru Airfield. An Imperial Navy airfield was located on Oroku Peninsula. Two airfields were located on Ie Shima.

Before the invasion 80,000 Okinawans were shipped to Kyushu aboard returning supply ships to work in factories (some were sunk en route by US submarines). Another 60,000 were forced to relocate to the sparse north, reducing the burden on Japanese forces in the heavily populated south.

Temperatures are moderate with a winter night low of 40°F (4.4°C)[6]. At the time of the battle, day temperatures ranged from the 70s to the 80s (degrees fahrenheit). Humidity is high all year around. Rain is frequent, but irregular, with the heaviest occurring from May to September during the summer monsoon – 93 in. (23.6 cm) per year. Rain was to have a major impact on the coming battle. Moderate winds varied from south to east at the time of the battle. Between May and November one or two typhoons may pass Okinawa each month.

Japanese and Okinawans lay claim to the same basic racial origins – the Ainu aborigines – but Okinawans have more Mongoloid and Malayan blood. Okinawans bear a physical resemblance to the Japanese, but there the similarity ends. Their languages have the same roots, but are mutually unintelligible (Japanese was taught in schools, but few Okinawans were proficient). The native language is Luchuan. Bearing extensive Chinese influence, Okinawa's culture and religion were distinctly different from Japan's. Furthermore, the Japanese viewed the Okinawans as inferior and there was wide disparity between the two races socially, economically, and politically, resulting in much resentment. Japanese on the island enjoyed many privileges not conferred on Okinawans. This secondary status did not, however, exempt Okinawans from military conscription to serve the Emperor. The coming battle for Okinawa could be described as a clash between three cultures, the effects of which still reverberate today. Ryukuans caught in the American storm sweeping across Okinawa would refer to the assault as the *tetsu no bofu*– "Typhoon of Steel."

---

1 Formosa was defended by 479,313 troops of the 10th Area Army under General Rikuchi Ando with the 9th, 12th, 50th, 66th, and 71st Divisions, 8th Air Division, 1st Air Fleet (IJN), and 12th, 75th, 76th, 102nd, and 103rd IMBs.
2 The existence of two "sub-theater" commanders in the Pacific Theater caused numerous conflicts and difficulties. It prevented complete unity of command and even made logistics distribution difficult. It was a political arrangement due to the personalities involved. The Twentieth Air Force's strategic B-29 bombers were directed by the Joint Chiefs of Staff rather than one of the service commanders to prevent either from appearing to possess a further strategic reach than the other.
3 In May 1944, the Pacific Fleet was reorganized to allow the Third and Fifth Fleets to be rotated, thus accelerating the war's tempo. One fleet planned, refitted, and trained for the next operation while the other fought. There was no decrease in operational tempo since as soon as one fleet had completed an operation, the other immediately went into action. The Fast Carrier Force, however, operated almost continuously and would be assigned to the operational fleet, although individual ships were rotated as required.
4 Translations of Japanese terms are: Shoto – groups of islands, Retto – archipelago, Gunto – group, Shima and Jima– island. Terms for settlements are: shi – city, sho – town, mura – village. Ryukyu is derived from the Chinese Liuchiu ("loochoo"), meaning something like "precious floating stones on the horizon" (almost every source gives a different meaning), and the Japanese inability to pronounce "L" resulted in Ryukyu.
5 The beaches were named after centrally located Hagushi Village at the mouth of the Bishi Gawa (stream). Hagushi, however, was actually a mistranslation. The village's real name was Togushi. The Japanese called them the Kadena Beaches.
6 Japanese forces were well supplied with warm clothing and blankets, while US troops were ill-prepared for the chilly nights.

CHRONOLOGY

1944

16–17 February, Task Force (TF) 58 aircraft strike and neutralize Truk.

15 June–9 July, V Amphibious Corps assaults and captures Saipan.

21 July–10 August, III Amphibious Corps assaults and captures Guam.

10 October, First carrier raid on Okinawa.

23–26 October, Japanese fleet is eliminated as a threat during the Battle of Leyte Gulf.

25 October, CinCPOA issues joint staff study for Operation *Iceberg*.

24 November, First B-29 bomber raid on Tokyo. Raid launched from Saipan.

1945

6 January, Tenth Army issues Tentative Operation Plan 1-45 for Operation *Iceberg*.

19 February–16 March, V Amphibious Corps assaults and captures Iwo Jima.

11 March (L-21), Tenth Army Operation Plan 1-45 put into effect.

21–27 March (L-11 to L-5), Operation *Iceberg* task forces and task groups sortie for Okinawa.

26–29 March (L-6 to L-3), 77th Inf. Div. assaults and captures Kerama Retto.

31 March (L-1), 420th Field Artillery Group lands on Keise Shima.

1 April (L-Day), Tenth Army assaults Okinawa's Hagushi Beaches with four divisions.

1–2 April, 2nd Mar. Div. conducts demonstrations off southwest coast.

2 April, Forward elements of 7th Inf. Div. reach east coast severing the island.

6/7 April, First of ten major *Kamikaze* attacks on TF 51 ships.

7 April, TF 58 aircraft sink battleship *Yamato* and four other warships.

6–11 April (L+5), 3rd Battalion, 105th Infantry secures Eastern Islands, Tsugen Shima on 10 April.

10 April, 27th Inf. Div. lands to reinforce XXIV Corps.

11 April, 2nd Mar. Div. (Tenth Army Floating Reserve) departs for Saipan.

16–21 April (W-Day), 77th Inf. Div. assaults and captures Ie Shima.

18 April, Ernie Pyle, the popular war correspondent, killed on Ie Shima.

19 April, XXIV Corps conducts major attack on outer Shuri defenses.

20 April, 6th Mar. Div. secures Motobu Peninsula in the north.

27 April, 77th Inf. Div. lands on Okinawa.

30 April, 77th Inf. Div. relieves 96th Inf. Div. in the south.

1 May, 1st Mar. Div. relieves 27th Inf. Div. in the south. The 1st is attached to XXIV Corps.

4 May, 27th Inf. Div. relieves 6th Mar. Div. in the north.

4–6 May, XXIV Corps repulses major Japanese counterattack.

7 May, III Amphibious Corps enters the southern line in the Tenth Army western sector and 1st Mar. Div. reattached to IIIAC.

8 May, 6th Mar. Div. enters the line in the south.

9 May, 96th Inf. Div. relieves 7th Inf. Div. in the south.

11 May, Tenth Army conducts major attack on inner Shuri defenses.

17 May, Admiral Turner relieved by Admiral Hill as Commander, TF 51. General Buckner now directly subordinate to Admiral Spruance, Commander, TF 50.

27 May, Third Fleet relieved Fifth Fleet (TF 51 becomes TF 31). General Buckner now directly subordinate to Admiral Nimitz, CinCPOA.

30 May, 8th Marines (Special Landing Force) returns from Saipan and secures unoccupied islands 3 and 9 June.

30 May–4 June, Japanese 32nd Army withdraws from Shuri defenses south to the Kiyamu Peninsula.

31 May, 5th Marines secure Shuri Castle.

4 June (K-Day), 4th Marines conduct shore-to-shore assault on Oroku Peninsula; last opposed amphibious assault in World War Two.

14 June, Marines secure Oroku Peninsula.

15 June, 8th Marines land at Naha and attach to 1st Mar. Div.

18 June, General Buckner killed. General Geiger (USMC) assumes command of Tenth Army.

21 June (L+82), End of organized resistance on Okinawa.

23 June, General Stillwell assumes command of Tenth Army.

26–30 June, Amphibious Reconnaissance Battalion, FMFPac assaults and secures Kume Shima; last amphibious assault in World War II.

30 June, Mopping-up of southern Okinawa completed.

1 July, TF 31 dissolved.

4 August, 27th Inf. Div. completes mopping-up of northern Okinawa.

6 August, Atomic bomb dropped on Hiroshima.

9 August, Atomic bomb dropped on Nagasaki.

10 August, Japan sues for peace.

14 August, Ceasefire in the Pacific Theater.

2 September (VJ-Day), Japan formally surrenders.

7 September, All remaining Japanese forces in the Ryukyus surrender.

POST-WAR

24 April 1946, Local government representation established on Okinawa by US Military Governor, Ryukyus.

15 May 1972, US Government returns Ryukyu Islands to Japanese Government control.

OPPOSING PLANS

THE JAPANESE PLAN

The great Japanese bastion on Truk in the Caroline Islands was neutralized by air in February 1944; a move followed by the fall of the crucial Mariana Islands (Saipan, Tinian, Guam) that summer. Heavily fortified Iwo Jima was seized in February and March 1945. All of the Pacific islands, taken in the glorious days of 1941 and early 1942, were now back in Allied hands or enduring the process of being bombed and strafed into submission. Only scattered remnants of the Imperial Japanese Army (IJA) (*Kogun*) held out in the Philippines. Much of the Imperial Japanese Navy (IJN) (*Kaigun*) rested on the bottom of the Pacific. Its once feared carrier air arm had virtually ceased to exist. US submarines had cut Japan's sea lanes. B-29 bombers rained explosives and incendiaries on Japan's teaming cities at will.

Expecting attacks on Formosa and the Ryukyus, Japan prepared to battle the Americans to a stalemate. Hoping that Japanese spirit would endure massed American firepower and limitless material resources, she strove to inflict unacceptable losses and sue for peace.

Nicknamed the *Baka* (Japanese for Fool) bomb by the Americans, the Imperial Japanese Navy's Yokosuka MXY-7 *Ohka* (Cherry Blossom) rocket-propelled bomb was dropped from a Mitsubishi "Betty" G4M twin-engine attack bomber and flown by a pilot into enemy ships. It had a range of 43 miles (69 km) carrying a 1,200-kg warhead, shown here with the nose piece removed. It had a 16 ft (5 m) wingspan and length of 20 ft (6.07 m). Only a few reached their targets as the mother aircraft were often shot down, but those that hit a ship sank it or inflicted major damage. Their 533 mph (860 km/h) speed and small size made them difficult to down with gunfire.

Japan began the Pacific War with a light infantry-based doctrine and concepts "validated" by combat in China against an ill-armed, poorly supplied, weakly led and disunited army. The initial onslaught into the Pacific and Southeast Asia against little or unprepared opposition only strengthened the illusion of the superiority of Japanese doctrine and military abilities.

The Japanese concept of warfare focused on the offensive spirit of *Bushido*. This doctrine, approaching religious fervor, was applied to the defense of Pacific islands. Its early failure in the Solomons and New Guinea forced a reluctant change. As observed in the Tenth US Army's

19

This 100-ft (30-m) long heavily log-reinforced tunnel had five rooms branching off it. The tunnel was found on Ie Shima, but was typical of those on the main island. They served as troop shelters during bombardments, housed command posts, aid stations, ammunition, and supplies. (USMC)

G-2 Intelligence Monograph of August 1945, "an army trained to attack on any and every occasion, irrespective of conditions, and with no calculation as to the real chances of success, could be beaten soundly." The concept of "impregnable defenses" was behind attempts to destroy the attackers on the beaches, but it proved a failure and was also unsuccessful in the Gilberts, Marshalls, and Marianas. The supposedly impenetrable beach obstacles and dense fortifications, designed to stop the attackers at the water's edge, were crushed by overwhelming American esprit de corps, firepower, and materiel. The senseless *banzai* charges, intended as local counterattacks to drive back a demoralized enemy, served only to hasten the inevitable end as Japanese soldiers died en masse for the Emperor under devastating American firepower.

A third defense strategy was introduced on Peleliu and then Iwo Jima. It sought to prolong the action and gradually grind down the attacking Americans as they battered themselves against heavily fortified defensive lines established in depth across the island. The goal was to inflict the maximum losses of troops, ships, aircraft, and material. It was to wear down the enemy's morale and break his spirit. There were no *banzai* charges on Peleliu or Iwo Jima and none were seen on Okinawa. The 32nd Army's battle slogan expressed this tactic in blunt terms:

One plane for one warship
One boat for one ship
One man for ten of the enemy or one tank

In February 1944, after Truk was blasted into impotence, plans for the *Ten–Go* Operation were laid. Japan reinforced the defenses of Formosa and Okinawa and established the 32nd Army on the latter in April. *Ten-Go* envisioned a network of inter-supporting air bases to destroy American air and sea forces venturing into their zones. Thirteen groups of air bases were established in the Ryukyu chain and on Formosa. A group of bases might contain three to five airfields defended by anti-aircraft guns and the islands by strong IJA garrisons. Multiple airfields in a group allowed damaged ones to be repaired and aircraft to use the remaining fields.

Ten–Go was suspended after the Marianas fell and a new plan, *Sho–Go 2*, instituted. It called for massive air attacks by aircraft swarming from the Home Islands, Formosa, and the Philippines if the Ryukyus were attacked. The 32nd Army on Okinawa was reinforced through the summer to boast three infantry divisions, an independent mixed brigade, and substantial support and service troops. The 32nd received a blow in November when the 9th Division, its best, was withdrawn for duty on Leyte[8]. Additional forces were sent to other Nansai Shoto islands[9] further diluting the defenses of Okinawa.

Only 30 aircraft remained on Okinawa, although extensive air service establishments existed. Most aircraft had been withdrawn to Formosa and Kyushu. Those few remaining were destroyed by US air and naval gunfire by early March. In February 1945, IJA Air Service (*Kokygun*) air regiments of the 6th Air Army and IJN Air Force (*Koku Buntai*) air groups were consolidated into the Combined Air Fleet under an IJN admiral. Besides massed conventional air attacks, invading Americans would face the *Kamikaze*, the "Divine Wind," or Special Attack (*Tokko*) as the Japanese designated them[10]. They were codenamed *Kikusui* (floating chrysanthemums). American naval forces first experienced *Kamikaze* attacks mounted as a last resort by the IJN in the Philippines.

The plans for the defense of Okinawa went through several iterations before that which the Americans faced was adopted. While the Imperial General Headquarters advocated a policy of "decisive battle" to aggressively attack the enemy in close combat and defend the island's airfields, the 32nd Army faced reality and chose to pursue a "war of attrition" (*Jikyusen*). Even with the arrival of the promised 84th Division in January to replace the 9th Division, the 32nd Army could not have defended the entire island, even though that course of action was desired by IGHQ. The 84th never arrived and the 32nd Army possessed the resources to defend only approximately one-third of the island. Two options were quickly rejected. The 10th Area Army on Formosa, to which 32nd Army was subordinate, desired the defense of the central plains with the Yontan and Kadena Airfields. Lieutenant-General Ushijima knew that with the arrival of the American fleet the airfields could not be used and his 32nd Army would be quickly destroyed on the exposed plains. Moving the 32nd Army to the rugged north might ensure, or at least prolong, its survival. But, this option would deprive it of its resources in the south and prevent it from forcing the Americans into close combat and inflicting unacceptable losses on them. The north lacked a viable road network and the 32nd Army did not have the transportation means to move what it needed into the northern hills.

To appease 10th Area Army, Ushijima thinly deployed the 44th Independent Mixed Brigade (IMB) to defend the central plains in December 1944. His two divisions were in the south. Ushijima's operations officer, Colonel Yahara, studied the deployment of the Army's units and felt they were still stretched too thin. By doctrine, a

OVERLEAF
KAMIKAZE BOATS AT NAHA
Q-boats, also known as *Renraku-tei* (liaison boats) as a cover designation, were 18 ft long and 5 ft wide. Their 85-horsepower, 6-cylinder Chevrolet engine gave them a 20-knot speed, which was not particularly fast, and a 3¹/₂-hour range. The cheaply constructed plywood boats carried a 551 lb (225 kg) explosive charge inside the bow. Some had a rack on either side of the cockpit for a 264 lb depth charge intended for dropping within 5 yards of a ship after making a U-turn to allow an escape. Battalion-size sea raiding regiments, code-named *Akatsuki* (dawn), consisted of an 11-man headquarters and three 31-man companies, each with three nine-man platoons and nine boats. A 900-man base battalion with mechanics and service personnel supported each regiment. The boats were hidden in caves or other camouflaged shelters and moved to launching ramps on a two-wheel cart. The 16–17-year old volunteers were 2nd and 3rd year officer cadets in the five-year officer academy. If one failed to return from his mission, he was presumed successful and posthumously promoted to lieutenant. The hoped for "blasting to pieces" of the American fleet by "whirlwind" Q-boat attacks never materialized. Numerous boats sortied, but were intercepted by "flycatcher" patrols of PT boats and an alert shipboard watch. They only managed to sink an LCI(G) and damage two destroyers and an LCS(L). (Howard Gerrard)

A heavily constructed concrete, limestone, and log bunker line on Mezado Ridge 500–600 yds (455–546 m) southwest of Kunishi and 1,200 yds (1,092 m) south of Itoman, 21 June. While used as bomb shelters, an embrasure was provided for a light machine-gun. Only a direct hit by a large-caliber projectile or a heavy bomb would breach such bunkers. (US Army)

Japanese division defended a six-mile (9.6-km) front. Ushijima's two divisions and single brigade actively defended 24 miles (39 km) and covered a further 12 miles (19 km) of cross-island and coastal defenses. The Americans would pour through such a broad, thinly held front. To shorten the fronts Yahara withdrew the 44th IMB from the central plains in January 1945 and assigned it some of the 62nd Division's sector.

IGHQ insisted that the Americans, after their Marianas victory, would first seize small Daito Jima 180 miles (240 km) to the east as a base of operations and wished it heavily defended. Yahara felt the Americans would not bother, but would instead strike straight at Okinawa. He rightfully resisted the effort to squander forces on the insignificant rock.

The 32nd Army's deployment found the 62nd Division covering an area in the south from Naha and Shuri north to a line anchored on the east and west coasts on the second narrowest neck of the island, the three-and-a-half mile (5.5-km) wide Chatan Isthmus. This north-facing front was dug in on some of the first high ground encountered south of the central plains where the Americans would land. A more formidable defense line behind this was centered on the rugged 4,500-yd (4.1-km) long Urasoe–Mura Escarpment, Tanabaru Escarpment, and several ridges running from northwest to southeast across the island. The main defense line, however, was still further south and centered on Shuri Castle and a vast, rugged cross-island ridge and hill complex. Forces on this line were withheld from the first week's fighting. The weary advancing Americans would run headlong into well-prepared and formidable defenses. The 24th Division secured the southern end of the island to prevent landings and act as the 32nd Army reserve. The 44th IMB was southeast of the 62nd defending the Chinen Peninsula, where it was thought the Americans might land on the island's southeast Minatogawa Beaches (Minatoga in most US documents). The Okinawa

Naval Base Force secured the Oroku Peninsula southwest of the 62nd Division and was prepared to fight the Americans at the water's edge as was IJN doctrine. The island's north was not completely abandoned. The 1st Specially Established Regiment (formed from airfield service personnel) screened the Yontan and Kadena Airfields on the central plains. The regimental-size 2nd Infantry Unit, detached from the 44th IMB, was established on the Motobu Peninsula on the island's northwest coast to distract the Americans and tie up forces. One of its battalions was on Ie Shima just west of the Motobu along with other small elements. All of the main units in Okinawa Gunto would be augmented by specially established units formed from service troops in March in a further effort to thicken the 32nd Army's overextended lines.

The 32nd Army had little faith in promised Japanese air support. In order to survive and slow the Americans to the maximum extent, the Army would dig. Thousands of pillboxes, bunkers, weapons emplacements, and fighting positions were dug. Terrain features were incorporated into the defense and weapons were well-sited with excellent overlapping fields of fire. Multiple defense lines were established across the island anchored on dominating terrain. The construction and improvement of these repeating lines would continue through the battle as the Japanese were painfully pushed south. Supplies and munitions were protected in dugouts and caves. Extensive tunnel systems were dug, over 60 miles (96.54 km), enough to protect the Army's 100,000 troops.

The Imperial Japanese Army provided four battalion-size sea-raiding regiments each with 100 *Kamikaze* boats in the Kerama Retto. They were to launch night suicide attacks on the invading fleet. It was a tactic first used in the Philippines, and considerable faith was misplaced in it.

When this plan was proposed, the 10th Area Army ordered Ushijima's chief of staff, Major-General Cho, to justify why the airfields were to be left virtually undefended and the doctrine of destroying the invaders on the beaches ignored. Cho argued that previous events had proven it was impossible to destroy an American landing force at the water's edge, that the airfields would be untenable, and their defense would only expose the 32nd Army leading to its early annihilation. Let the Americans land where they chose, but once ashore and with little room to maneuver, they would encounter dug-in defenses on coast-to-coast ridge lines defended by an army prepared to maneuver and attack the enemy in a decisive battle. The 10th Area Army, to appease Ushijima for the self-serving withdrawal of the 9th Division, offered no more resistance to the plan.

Cho also flew to Tokyo in January for a final conference on the defense of Okinawa. He was told that *Kamikaze* air and sea attacks would be the sole means of destroying the American fleet. Imperial Japanese Army artillery and coast defense guns would hold their fire so as not to reveal their positions. They would be preserved to engage the Americans ashore when they became intermingled among the dense Japanese defenses. This would also help negate American air and naval gunfire support, the power of which the Japanese fully appreciated after recent battles.

A few weeks before the invasion, the 32nd Army was alerted by the Imperial General Headquarters that Admirals King and Nimitz had held a conference in Washington in early March. The Japanese had found that new operations occurred from 20–30 days after such high-level strategy conferences were held. Formosa or Okinawa was identified as the likely target.

However, any fortified defensive line, be it the Maginot, Gothic, *Westwall*, or the dug-in 32nd Army, can be defeated.

THE AMERICAN PLAN

The Joint Expeditionary Force (Task Force 51) faced a daunting challenge when plans for *Iceberg* began to be developed. First, intelligence on the area had to be collected. Accurate maps and sea charts were not available. The initial photo-mapping mission was flown during B-29 strikes in September 1944. All of Okinawa was photographed as were many of the outlying islands. Most of the north of the island, however, was hidden by clouds. Contour lines from captured Japanese maps were overprinted on the white areas, but it was not until midway through the campaign that complete photo-maps were available. Additional photo coverage, including photos of specific target areas, was obtained during the October carrier strikes.

American estimates of enemy strength and disposition were moderately accurate and erred on the low side. Estimates were revised over the months prior to the landing as the Japanese 9th Division was withdrawn and small numbers of reinforcements arrived on supply ships. By March 1945 it was estimated that 75,000 troops organized into 2½ divisions were on the island. It was understood that the enemy were concentrated on the southern third of the island and preparing a defense in-depth. As on Guam, a small force screened the north. Like the Japanese, the Americans felt this was more effective than a water's edge defense and potentially more dangerous to the landing force. They did, however, contemplate more resistance on the beaches than Ushijima had prepared and expected up to 80 percent casualties among the assault troops.

Initial planning began in September 1944 and called for a three-phase operation. The plan assumed that B-29s bombing Japan from the Marianas, the seizure of Iwo Jima, and carrier strikes on the Home Islands would concentrate all available Japanese aircraft there. The Okinawa landings would provoke violent air attacks on the fleet. One of the plan's main goals was the early seizure of the Yontan and Kadena Airfields for land-based aircraft to protect the fleet and provide close air support. The original plan preferred the west-coast beaches, but Admiral Turner expressed reservations because of expected winds and high surf conditions on 1 March. The east-coast Nakagusuka Wan (Bay) beaches were less favorable and the operation's postponement to April dispelled his concerns about the west-coast beaches.

Phase I called for the early securing of southern Okinawa and the development of its airfields along with seizing many of the offshore islands. The seizure of Ie Shima (codenamed *Indispensable*) and the rest of Okinawa was to take place in Phase II, and additional islands in the Ryukyus would also be seized. In Phase III Kikai Shima north of Okinawa was to be seized by 1st Mar. Div. and Miyako Shima in Sakishima Gunto near Formosa by V Amphibious Corps. In fact, V

From left to right: Admiral Raymond A. Spruance, Commander, Central Pacific Task Forces and Fifth Fleet; Fleet Admiral Chester W. Nimitz, Commander-in-Chief, Pacific Ocean Areas; and Lieutenant-General Simon B. Buckner Jr., Commanding General, Tenth Army. (USMC)

This formidable defensive position, made from reinforced concrete approximately 2 ft (60 cm) thick, utilizes a converted cave. Similar multiple positions and other, simpler fighting positions covered each other along limestone ridge lines. The larger embrasure could accommodate a light or heavy-machine gun while the smaller upper firing-slit allowed a rifleman to provide close-in protection and spot targets for the machine gunner whose vision might be obscured by dust. The "stepped" design of the embrasure helped prevent bullets from ricocheting into the opening. The 5-gal. (23-litre) water can was included in the photograph to give a sense of scale. Torn tree limbs in front originally camouflaged the position, which was connected to others by caves and tunnels. This position was near Beach "Yellow 2" in the 1st Marine Division's sector. (USMC)

Amphibious Corps was too badly mauled at Iwo Jima to undertake the operation. In the final plan, approved on 6 January 1945, Phase III was eliminated due to logistical considerations and Phases I and II were reversed, but the seizure of other islands was later canceled.

The new Phase I called for the early capture of Kerama Retto, 15 miles (24 km) west, by the 77th Inf. Div. beginning almost a week before the main landing. Kerama Retto would provide an ideal anchorage for refueling, rearming, and repairing ships of the bombardment line. A seaplane base for anti-submarine patrols was to be established there as well. One day before the main landing, an Army infantry battalion would secure Keise Shima, 11 miles (18 km) southwest of the Hagushi Beaches, and a field artillery group's long-range guns emplaced for fire support. An elaborate deception operation was to begin off the southeast coast of Okinawa two days before the Kerama Retto operation. Minesweepers, covered by fighters, would clear the waters while battleships bombarded positions ashore. The 2nd Mar. Div. would reinforce this deception by demonstrating off the beaches in hope the Japanese would rush reinforcements to the south and tie down counterattack forces that could be used against the real landing. Air strikes on Kyushu airfields would delay Japanese air attacks from the Home Islands.

The main landing would begin at 0830hrs, 1 April 1945, H-Hour, L-Day. The largest simultaneous amphibious assault in the Pacific War would see the landing of two Marine and two Army divisions abreast on eight miles (12.8 km) of beach. III Amphibious Corps (IIIAC) would land opposite Yontan Airfield with its 6th Mar. Div. on the left. The Division would move rapidly inland, seize the airfield and protect Tenth

Army's north flank by severing the island at the narrow Ishikawa Isthmus. Its 22nd Marines would land on the left flank. The 4th Marines would land on the right, its 2nd Battalion in Division Reserve, and would focus on the airfield. The Division's 29th Marines was in IIIAC Reserve to land to order. On the IIIAC's right, the 1st Marine Division would storm ashore south of the airfield and maintain contact with XXIV Corps on its right. The 7th Marines would land on the Division's left and the 5th on the right. The 1st Marines would be in Division Reserve and follow the 7th ashore. IIIAC Artillery would land on order in two groups of three battalions, with one group supporting each division. The Eastern Islands would be secured as required to further protect Tenth Army's seaward eastern flank.

The Bishi Gawa (stream) served as the initial physical boundary between IIIAC and XXIV Corps. The veteran 7th Infantry Division would land on the Corps' left, maintain contact with IIIAC, and seize Kadena Airfield. Its 17th Infantry would be on the left and the 32nd on the right. The 184th Infantry was the Division Reserve. The 96th Inf. Div. would land south of the airfield with its 381st Infantry on the left and the 383rd Infantry on the right. Its 382nd Infantry was the Corps Reserve. There was no division reserve, but the 382nd would land behind the 381st and be prepared to respond to a Japanese counterattack from the south. XXIV Artillery (less the group on Keise Shima) would land as necessary to support the Corps attack. The Corps' main mission, after capturing Kadena Airfield, was to swing south and secure an eastwest line through Kuba Saki and seal off the Japanese in the south.

The 2nd Mar. Div., after conducting its demonstration off the southeast beaches, would remain as the Tenth Army Floating Reserve along with the 27th Inf. Div. as the Expeditionary Troops Floating Reserve. The 81st Inf. Div. was held on New Caledonia as the Area Reserve.

Once the island was severed and the Japanese forces divided and isolated, the central portion of the island secured, and logistical build-up under way, XXIV Corps would advance south with the 7th Inf. Div. on the left (east) and the 96th on the right (west) to seize the main objective area; the island's southern end. IIIAC would back up XXIV Corps, securing the occupied sector across the island with its 1st Mar. Div. while the 6th advanced to clear the north end of the island. The 77th Inf. Div. would seize Ie Shima when ordered. The 27th Inf. Div., would land as necessary as XXIV Corps' frontline lengthened as the advance pressed south to where the island widened.

Initial air support for the landing forces would be provided by 14 escort carriers. Over 220 Marine fighters of Tactical Air Force, Tenth Army, a joint air force under Marine command, would be moved ashore from four escort carriers as airfields were captured and developed. Additional shore-based aircraft would be staged ashore at a later date.

The Navy task forces assigned to Task Force 51 would transport and deliver the landing forces, sustain them ashore, provide air cover and close air support, and deliver naval gunfire support. The Fifth Fleet's Fast Carrier Striking Force (TF 58) and British Carrier Force (TF 57) would attack Japanese air bases in the Home Islands, on Formosa, and the Ryukyus. They would also be prepared to engage any remnants of the Imperial Fleet that might attempt to sortie. Over 1,300 ships were committed to Operation *Iceberg*. Twentieth Air Force B-29 bombers would continue their pounding of Japan, especially air bases, and the Pacific Fleet Submarine Force would establish a barrier between Japan and Okinawa.

The logistic effort to mount and sustain such a massive campaign was enormous. Participating units staged at Espíritu Santo, Guadalcanal, the Russells, Saipan, Guam, Eniwetok, New Caledonia, Leyte, Oahu, and the West Coast of the United States. They formed up at Ulithi over 1,000 miles (1,609 km) to the southeast of Okinawa while other forces moved directly from Leyte. Just the effort and resources required to support all these far flung bases and maintain a supply line 4,000 miles (6,437 km) and 17 days steaming from Pearl Harbor – 6,200 miles (9,978 km), 26 days steaming from the West Coast – were phenomenal. The ability of the landing beaches to receive troops and supplies and availability of shipping were other governing factors. A total of 458 ships were required to transport and support the landing forces. Ammunition expenditure rates would be so high, over three times that used in the Marianas, that shortages were experienced from the West Coast all the way across the Pacific. Four major airfields would be constructed on Okinawa, requiring an effort much more than simply capturing existing crude strips. The new fields would be more extensive and the construction projects would literally change the island's landscape. The port of Naha would be rebuilt and expanded, and a massive advanced fleet operating base established at Nakagusuku Wan on the east side. Bases and facilities would be constructed from which to launch an even larger operation – the invasion of Japan.

---

7 Literally Bushi (warrior), Do (way or moral doctrine), i.e., "way of the warrior."
8 The 9th Division was actually sent to Formosa under the 32nd Army's superior, 10th Area Army, a self-serving act still bitterly debated among Japanese historians.
9 These forces were deployed to defend the Amami Gunto with the 21st IMR on Amami O Shima and 64th IMB on Tokuno Shima. The Sakishima Gunto was defended by the 28th Division and 60th IMB on Miyako Jima, 59th IMB on Irabu Jima, and 45th IMB on Ishigaki Jima.
10 While Westerners are intrigued and baffled by the Kamikaze concept, it was practical and honorable to the Japanese. Koku Buntai Captain Rikibei Inoguchi explained, "We must give our lives to the Emperor and Country, this is our inborn feeling. We Japanese base our lives on obedience to Emperor and Country. On the other hand, we wish for the best place in death, according to Bushido. Kamikaze was the incarnation of these feelings."

OPPOSING COMMANDERS

AMERICAN COMMANDERS

Task Force 50, the Fifth Fleet and Central Pacific Task Forces, was a joint command in the purest definition. This is reflected in its senior commanders, who represented the US Navy, Army, Marine Corps, and those services' air arms. By the time of the battle for Okinawa, the committed US forces had been forged into an efficient fighting machine capable of defeating any foe challenging them. Of all the many factors contributing to this skill at arms – planning, intelligence, training, logistics, and materiel resources – the diversified experiences of the task force's commanders was paramount.

The American system of command allowed a remarkable degree of latitude to subordinate commanders at all levels. Higher commanders developed strategic plans, after a great deal of coordination to accommodate the capabilities and limitations of each service. Their staffs refined the plans' details and allocated combat forces and logistics to execute the mission. Subordinate commanders and their staffs then developed their own operational and tactical plans to accomplish the mission. How they allocated and employed their own forces was, with some minor exceptions, left entirely to them. This degree of freedom

Troops of the 1st Mar. Div. board a landing craft, vehicle and personnel (LCVP) alongside an assault transport on the morning of L-Day. Rather than the rope cargo nets used earlier, these men have the benefit of more stable chain and wooden rung ladders. An LCVP, the most used landing craft, could carry 36 troops or a 6,000-lb (2,722-kg) vehicle or 8,100 lb (3,674 kg) of cargo. The 35-ft 9-in. (11-m) craft were armed with two .30cal. M1919A4 machine guns. (USMC)

Assault troops of the 1st Mar. Div. churn ashore aboard a landing vehicle, tracked Mk 3 (LVT[3]) amphibian tractor. This view is toward the Amtrac's stern and shows a .50cal. HB-M2 machine gun. Five-gallon (23-litre) water cans line the Amtrac's sides for use ashore and for protection from small-arms fire. (USMC)

was seldom realized in any other nations' armed forces. It was not uncommon for a senior commander to disagree with a subordinate's employment of his forces, but, generally, so long as the mission could be accomplished and the plan supported the overall plan, it was executed as the subordinate commander desired. It typified a basic American trait, "Tell me what needs to be done, then let me do it."

Raymond A. Spruance graduated from the Naval Academy in 1906 serving on battleships, then commanding destroyers, and finally a battleship in 1938–39. In the 1920s he served on numerous staffs in such varied disciplines as engineering and intelligence. His early operational experience saw him as Commander, Caribbean Sea Frontier, where he dealt with a potentially hostile Vichy French force and marauding U-boats attacking Allied shipping. The US entry into the war found him in command of a cruiser division, which escorted the USS *Hornet* during Doolittle's Tokyo raid. He commanded a two-carrier task force during the Battle of Midway and sank four Japanese carriers, inflicting a crippling blow on Japan. In rapid succession he became Nimitz's chief-of-staff, deputy commander of the Pacific Fleet, and then took command of the Central Pacific Force, which became the Fifth Fleet. In that capacity he directed Army and Marine forces seizing the Gilberts, Marshalls (after his promotion to admiral), and Marianas; some of the most complex joint amphibious operations to date. Forces under his command were victorious in the Battle of the Philippine Sea. The Fifth Fleet had grown into arguably the world's most powerful fleet. Spruance went on to seize Iwo Jima in February 1945 and then marshaled his forces for the final battle. As Commander, Task Force 50, Fifth Fleet and Central Pacific Task Forces, Spruance executed the largest amphibious operation of the war. He went on to command the Pacific Fleet after the war, but soon relinquished command to become president of the Naval War College. Retiring in 1948, he later served as ambassador to the Philippines. He died in 1969.

Richmond K. Turner graduated from the Naval Academy two years after his immediate superior at Okinawa, Spruance. Turner served on

LEFT **A soldier is treated by his buddies. He was one of the 104 wounded suffered on L-Day. Note that the soldier to the far left wears a Browning automatic rifle belt holding 12 20-round magazines. (US Army)**

BELOW **Troops of the 32nd Infantry, 7th Inf. Div. rest during the push inland toward Kadena Airfield from the "Orange" Beaches, 1 April. The man in the foreground carries an M2 tripod for a .30cal. M1919A4 machine gun and a 250-round M1 ammunition can. A gas mask case and M1910 pick-mattock are on his left hip. The flame gunner behind him carries an M2-2 flamethrower. (US Army)**

battleships during the Great War, but in 1926 he made a major career change and was rated a Naval Aviator. Numerous aviation staff assignments followed, including as executive officer of the carrier USS *Saratoga* and culminating as Commander, Aircraft, Battle Force for the US Fleet. He next commanded a cruiser and then attended the Naval War College. The opening shots of the war found him as director of the Navy Department's War Plans Division. In the summer of 1942 Turner took over command of amphibious forces in the South Pacific. His experience on planning staffs and the command of air units and ships of the line were to serve him well as he launched the grueling Solomon Islands campaign. Here he experienced his only defeat during the Savo Island Battle. In August 1943, he assumed command of Admiral Spruance's amphibious forces to perfect landing force operations in the Gilberts, Marshalls (after promotion to vice-admiral), Marianas, and Iwo Jima. As Commander, Joint Expeditionary Force (TF 51), during the Okinawa landings, Turner directed all amphibious forces of the Third and Fifth Fleets. He was promoted to admiral in May 1945 while the battle still raged. After the war he served as the US Navy representative to the UN Military Staff Committee until retiring in 1947. Turner died in 1961.

Simon B. Buckner, Jr., the son of a Confederate general, attended the Virginia Military Institute before acceptance to the Military Academy at West Point. Graduating in 1908, he served as an infantry officer alternating mainly between Mexican border duty and the Philippines. In 1917 he, like his future commander, became an aviator. He spent little time in the air, however, as he attended the Infantry School, Command and General Staff College (C&GSC), and Army War College. Between schools he served as an instructor at each as well as at West Point. In the late 1930s he commanded infantry regiments and served on a division staff. In 1940 he took command of US forces in Alaska. In 1942 he countered Japanese landing attempts in the Aleutians and retook the islands they had seized by the next summer. He was promoted to

A landing craft, infantry (gun) (LCI[G]) type D. It mounts five 4.5-in. Mk 7 rocket launchers on either side along with three 40-mm and four 20-mm guns. Each Mk 7 launcher rack holds 12 high explosive rockets with a range of 1,100 yds (1,006 m). These craft preceded the assault waves toward shore firing suppressive barrages. Three of the same Mk 7 launcher racks were mounted on Marine 1-ton trucks. (USMC)

lieutenant-general in May 1943 and remained in command in Alaska until June 1944. Ordered to Hawaii, Buckner organized and took command of the Tenth Army. He quickly welded his new joint Army/Marine command into an effective force and led it to Okinawa as Commanding General, Expeditionary Troops and Tenth Army (TF 56). Three days before the island was declared secure, Buckner was killed observing his troops' advance on the final organized resistance.

While the most senior commanders of Operation *Iceberg* were products of the service academies, **John R. Hodge** received a Reserve Officers Training Corps commission from the University of Illinois in 1917. Soon receiving a regular commission in the infantry, he served in France in 1918–19. He taught military science at a college before attending the Infantry School and then served in Hawaii. In the mid-1930s he attended C&GSC and the Army War College. The Pearl Harbor attack found Hodge on the VII Corps staff. As assistant commander of the 25th Inf. Div. he fought on Guadalcanal alongside the Marines. Promoted to major-general in April 1943, he took command of the bloodied American Division leading it at Bougainville. His next assignment was commander of XXIV Corps in April 1944. Under the Sixth Army and landed by the Seventh Fleet in October, Hodge led his corps through the bitter Leyte campaign to secure the island by the year's end. Besides his experience with the Marines on Guadalcanal and Bougainville, the Marine V Amphibious Corps Artillery supported him on Leyte (while his own XXIV Corps Artillery supported the Marines on Saipan and Tinian). Returned to Hawaii, XXIV Corps joined the new Tenth Army to prepare for the assault on Okinawa. At the war's end Lieutenant-General Hodge led his corps to Korea for occupation duty. From 1948 he held further corps and army commands until retirement in 1953. He died ten years later.

Roy S. Geiger was considered an oddity by many – he was a Naval Aviator[11], the fifth Marine to become a pilot, and an amphibious corps commander. He flew in and commanded Marine aviation units from 1917 right up to assuming command of I Marine Amphibious Corps in November 1943. Geiger enlisted in the Marine Corps in 1907 after graduating from college. He was commissioned an infantry officer two years later to serve in Central America, China, and elsewhere. Between major aviation commands he attended the Army's C&GSC and War College, and then the Naval War College. In August 1941, Geiger took command of the 1st Marine Aircraft Wing taking it to Guadalcanal where he was promoted to major-general. In May 1943, he was assigned as Director, Division of Aviation, Headquarters, Marine Corps. In November he took command of the 1st Marine Amphibious Corps, considered an unusual move by many due to his flying vocation. But he excelled in two areas critical to successful corps operations, fire support (artillery, naval, air) and logistics. He led the corps on Bougainville, then to Guam (the Corps was redesignated III Amphibious Corps in April 1944), and Peleliu. On both Guadalcanal and Bougainville Geiger worked with John R. Hodge, his future sister corps commander on Okinawa. With the death of Lieutenant-General Buckner on 18 June 1945, Geiger assumed command of Tenth Army, the only Marine officer to command a field army, while retaining command of IIIAC. The next day he was promoted to lieutenant-general. General Buckner had expressly picked Geiger to assume command in the event of his death. Five days later, Geiger was relieved by Lieutenant-General Joseph W. Stilwell. In July 1945 Geiger took command of Fleet Marine Force, Pacific. In late 1946 he was assigned to Headquarters, Marine Corps, but became ill just before his scheduled retirement and died in January 1947. Later in the year he was given posthumous promotion to full general by a grateful Congress.

JAPANESE COMMANDERS

The Imperial Headquarters appointed **Lieutenant-General Mitsuru Ushijima**[12] as commander of the Japanese 32nd Army on 8 August 1944. He arrived two days later to replace the ailing Lieutenant-General Masao Watanabe. A 1908 graduate of the Japanese Military Academy, Ushijima was an infantry officer who had progressed through the usual command and staff duties, eventually serving as a vice minister in the Ministry of the Army. In 1942 he commanded an infantry group in Burma, a brigade-equivalent command. His assignment to the 32nd Army relieved him from his duties as commandant of the Military Academy. Ushijima believed in mentoring his subordinates and rather than taking sides when his staff frequently disagreed as to a course of action, he resolved disputes through mediation. As a commander he was described as coolly appreciative of reality.

The steady and reserved Ushijima selected a very different individual as his chief-of-staff. **Major-General Isamu Cho** was known for his strong emotions, enthusiasm, and boldness. As a regimental commander in the 19th Division, he once napped on a hillside in full view of Soviet troops during the 1938 Manchuria border dispute. He enjoyed good food and drink, often performing a wild sword dance when sufficiently inebriated. Graduating from the Military Academy in 1916, he progressed rapidly, although his career was marred by involvement in

This aerial view of the beachhead on L+4 gives some idea of the logistical effort required to sustain a landing force ashore. Six Landing Ships, Tank (LST) are off-loading at center right of the picture. The reef prevents them from grounding closer to shore. The small bay above and to the left of the LSTs is the mouth of the Bishi Gawa (Stream). (USMC)

several coup attempts by the radical right-wing Cherry Society (Sakura-kai). In the 1931 coup attempt he was promised the position of police chief of Tokyo. His reward was banishment to China. There he helped plan the occupation of Manchuria and later the Marco Polo Bridge Incident in Peking. Serving as the chief-of-staff to Prince Yasuhiko Asaka (Emperor Hirohito's uncle) in 1937, he was responsible for relaying the prince's orders to massacre up to 300,000 Chinese in Nanking. He served on the Southern Army staff during the invasion of Burma and briefly commanded the 10th Division in Manchuria before being sent to the Philippines in 1942. Cho was finally allowed to return to Japan in 1944 to take part in the planned recapture of Saipan. When this operation was canceled, he was assigned to the Ministry of War's Military Affairs Bureau and then as the 32nd Army's chief-of-staff on 8 July 1944. He was promoted to lieutenant-general on 1 March 1945. Cho was the main advocate of the underground defense of Okinawa, but he was also responsible for the disastrous all-out May offensive. While widely different in background and temperament, the team of Ushijima and Cho has been compared to that of Hindenburg and Ludendorf.

While of comparatively junior rank, an equally important, and unique, member of the 32nd Army staff was **Colonel Hiromichi Yahara**, the senior operations officer. Yahara was an expert in developing operation plans and had long experience on staffs. A 1923 graduate of the Military Academy, where he later instructed, he served on staffs in

Used by both the Army and Marines, the 2½-ton amphibious truck or "Duck" (derived for their designation, DUKW-353) was mainly used to haul light-artillery pieces and ammunition ashore. They were able to move inland and deliver their cargo where necessary to prevent congestion on the beaches. Here a hoist-equipped D-9 dozer tractor unloads ammunition. (US Army)

China, Malaya, and Burma, and at the War Office. His higher military education included the Japanese War College and he spent two years as an exchange officer in the United States. Aloof and cool, he was widely recognized as an expert in his field. His personality was the exact opposite of Cho's, his immediate superior.

A Japanese staff functioned very differently from its Western counterpart. The commander bore the burden of spiritual responsibility, maintained contact with higher headquarters, and guided his staff. The chief-of-staff and operations officer possessed far more power than a Western chief-of-staff and G-3. Staff officers presented options to the chief and decisions were derived by negotiation, guided by the commander, to reach a common consensus. In reality, aggressive and opinionated staff officers, concerned with face-saving, often battled their way through planning sessions with factions of officers taking sides. Planning was made more difficult in an environment where anyone advising caution was branded a coward, where major commanders took complete operational freedom (*Dokudan Senko*) from higher headquarters, and subordinates often ignored their commanders (*Gekokujo*). It can be assumed that 32nd Army staff meetings were lively in an atmosphere where Cho's and Yahara's "discussions" were described as theatrical. Yahara was the most senior Japanese officer to survive the battle and wrote a book on his experiences.

---

11 Marine pilots were rated as Naval Aviators.
12 The Japanese place the surname first and the personal name second. Contemporary and post-war writings usually reversed the two. This book continues that practice. Many different spellings of Japanese names will be encountered due to interpretations of the two or more *Kanji* ideographs making up a man's name. The personal name of an adult male is almost never spoken with even close friends using a formal address. The actual meaning of the ideograph selected by a man's parents may not even be known to his closest friends.

OPPOSING FORCES

TASK FORCE 51

As a joint command, **Task Force 51** (TF 51), the Joint Expeditionary Force, contained elements from the US Army, Navy, Marine Corps, and the three services' air arms. It was a completely self-contained force capable of delivering itself to its area of operations, sustaining itself for 30 days, and executing combat actions in the air, on land, and on and under the sea. TF 51 was itself a component of another task force, TF 50, the Fifth Fleet and Central Pacific Forces under Admiral Raymond A. Spruance. Spruance, as the commander tasked with carrying out the invasion, directly controlled two other task forces participating in the Okinawa campaign.

The **Fast Carrier Force** (TF 58), under Vice-Admiral Marc A. Mitscher, had 88 ships including 11 fleet carriers and six light carriers with almost 1,400 aircraft backed by seven battleships, 18 cruisers, scores of destroyers and escorts, and a massive logistics support group. Vice-Admiral Sir Bernard Rawlings' **British Carrier Force** (TF 57) contributed four carriers, two battleships, five cruisers, and 14 destroyers plus a fleet train. Most of its 260 aircraft were American-built. Task Force 50 could also depend on support from other commands to include Submarine Force, Pacific Fleet; US Army Air Forces in China, and B-29s of the Twentieth Air Force flying out of the Marianas.

A D-18 bulldozer disembarks from a landing craft, tank Mk 6 (LCT[6]). Other engineer equipment will follow. The 119½-foot (36.4-m) long craft could carry four medium tanks or 150 tons of cargo. It was armed with two 20-mm guns. The stern could be opened and several LCTs could be anchored end-to-end to serve as a floating causeway between shore and an LST, as vehicles could simply drive through the connected craft. (US Army)

Task Force 51, the Joint Expeditionary Force, consisted of five smaller task forces and three task groups under Vice-Admiral Richmond K. Turner, Commander, Amphibious Forces, Pacific. Many of the Task Force's Navy units had little respite after the February Iwo Jima operation. This actually eased planning as command and communications systems had been battle-tested and refined. Task Force 51's command relationships, tasks, and subordinate forces were complex and are paraphrased here:

Amphibious Support Force (TF 52), Rear-Admiral William H.P. Blandy, included 18 escort carriers with 450 close air support aircraft in Support Carrier Group (TG 52.1), four more escort carriers (Special Escort Carrier Group) to deliver Marine Aircraft Groups 31 and 33 ashore, escorting destroyers, over 60 minesweepers (Mine Flotilla, TG 52.2) to clear approaches to the island, and ten 100-man underwater demolition teams (UDT) with each aboard a destroyer transport (Underwater Demolition Flotilla, TG 52.11) along with 170 fire support landing craft armed with guns, rockets, and mortars.

Western Islands Attack Group (TG 51.1), Rear-Admiral Ingolf N. Kiland, with the 77th Inf. Div. embarked, were to secure Kerama Retto and other offshore islands prior to L-Day. It was then to seize Ie Shima. It had 17 attack and attack cargo transports, 56 LSTs (Landing Ship, Tank), and numerous smaller support craft, destroyers, and escorts.

Northern Attack Force (TF 53), Rear-Admiral Lawrence F. Reifsnider, had two transport groups, each with over 20 attack and attack cargo transports with III Amphibious Corps' 1st and 6th Marine Divisions embarked. With them were 67 LSTs transporting amphibious tractors and pontoon causeways plus screening destroyers.

Gunfire and Covering Force (TF 54), Rear-Admiral Morton L. Deyo, would provide naval gunfire support with nine battleships, ten cruisers, and numerous destroyers.

Southern Attack Force (TF 55), Rear Admiral John L. Hall, was organized roughly the same as TF 53 , but with three transport groups. Embarked aboard these were XXIV Corps' 7th, 27th, and 96th Infantry Divisions. The 27th was TF 51's Floating Reserve (TG 51.3).

Demonstration Group (TG 51.2) consisted of a transport group carrying the 2nd Marine Division, the Tenth Army's Floating Reserve.

The **Expeditionary Troops** (TF 56) controlled all ground forces involved in the assault and the follow-on Island Command. In terms of manpower, it was the largest force within TF 50. Under the command of Lieutenant-General Simon B. Buckner, it was built around the Tenth Army.

US ARMY

Tenth Army was activated at Ft. Sam Houston, Texas, on 20 June 1944. It deployed to Schofield Barracks, Oahu, Hawaii, in August and prepared to assault Okinawa Gunto. Tenth Army was composed of two corps, one Army and the other Marine. It was unique in that it controlled its own tactical air force, a joint Marine and Army command. Tenth Army comprized over 102,000 Army troops of which over 38,000 were non-divisional artillery, combat support, and headquarters troops and some 9,000 service troops. Over 88,000 Marines were

A twin 40-mm antiaircraft gun mounted on an unidentified type of landing ship. The 40-mm Bofors was mounted on virtually all ships in either single, twin, or quad mountings (the latter two being liquid-cooled) for antiaircraft defense, which was essential at Okinawa because of the unrelenting *Kamikaze* attacks. Landing ships operating close inshore used antiaircraft guns to place suppressive fire on shore targets. Scores of four-round clips line the gun tub. (USMC)

assigned along with 18,000 Navy (mainly Seabees and medical personnel). Tenth Army assault troops, those landing in the initial assault, totaled 182,821 men.

Directly under Tenth Army was the **53rd Antiaircraft Artillery Brigade** with five AAA groups, six 90-mm and three 40-mm AAA battalions. All participating units had more than the usual allocation of AAA units due to Okinawa's proximity to Japan and Formosa. Additional military police (MP) and military government units were assigned in anticipation of an increased need to provide traffic control, guard prisoners of war and civilian internees, and conduct rear area security. This was due to lessons learned on Saipan and Tinian where the US first experienced large numbers of enemy civilians and refugees. Other troops included a medical group and signal units.

XXIV Corps (Southern Landing Force) was a relative late-comer in the Pacific. Activated at Ft. Shafter, Oahu, Hawaii, on 8 April 1944, it fought on Leyte from October to December with its 7th and 96th Infantry Divisions. It then secured undefended islands and prepared for Okinawa, departing Leyte at the end of March 1945. Under the command of Lieutenant-General John R. Hodge, the Corps already had valuable experience working with Marines. V Amphibious Corps (VAC) and XXIV Corps Artillery had been positioned to support the Yap Island assault, but this was canceled in August 1944. Due to unit positioning, VAC Artillery supported XXIV Corps on Leyte while XXIV Corps Artillery went with VAC to Saipan and Tinian.

XXIV Corps Artillery, under Brigadier-General Josef R. Sheetz, had three artillery groups with 14 battalions of various calibers. Okinawa saw the first use of the 8-in. howitzer in the Pacific. Rounding out the Corps was an engineer construction group, quartermaster group, medical group, and numerous combat support battalions.

Four infantry divisions were assigned to XXIV Corps. The reinforced 7th, 77th, and 96th averaged almost 22,000 troops, but each was some

The first Okinawan civilians are interned by Marine military policemen on 2 April. The Army and Navy dedicated almost 5,000 personnel to provide a military government organization, operate hospitals, and build and maintain 12 camps for the care of civilians, each housing up to 10,000 individuals. (USMC)

1,000 infantrymen understrength. Stateside replacement centers were unable to keep pace with the increasing tempo of the war in the Pacific and Europe. The divisions were reinforced by an engineer combat group for shore party duty, tank, amphibian tank, two amphibian tractor, and two AAA battalions plus additional medical units.

The Regular Army **7th Infantry Division** was reactivated (it had served in World War One) at Ft. Ord, California, on 1 July 1940. Its experiences were varied. After first receiving desert training, and then amphibious training from the Marines, it seized Attu Island in the Aleutians in May 1943. It moved to Hawaii and assaulted Kwajalein Atoll in January 1944. After returning to Hawaii, it fought on Leyte in October then prepared for Okinawa. The "Bayonet Division" was commanded by Major-General Archibald V. Arnold.

The **96th Infantry Division**, an Army Reserve unit, was activated at the end of World War One, but did not serve overseas. It was reactivated at Camp Adair, Oregon on 15 August 1942. After extensive training, which included amphibious training under the Marines, it assaulted Leyte in October 1944. The "Deadeye Division" was under the command of Major-General James L. Bradley for its entire World War Two service.

The **27th Infantry Division**, the floating reserve, would be the next to arrive on Okinawa. It fielded only just over 16,000 troops and was 2,000 infantrymen short. This was a New York National Guard unit and had served on the Mexican border in 1916 and fought in World War One. It was inducted into Federal service on 15 October 1940 in New York City and had a rather checkered relationship with the Marines. After training in the South, it moved to Hawaii and assaulted Saipan under VAC. Accused of excessive caution and lack of aggression, its commanding officer was relieved of command by the Marine VAC commander, souring Army-Marine relations. On Okinawa the "New York Division" was commanded by Major-General George W. Griner, Jr.

The last division to land on Okinawa, but the first to see combat in the Ryukyus, was the **77th Infantry Division**. Like the 96th, it was an Army Reserve division, but it had seen combat in World War One. It was reactivated on 25 March 1942 at Ft. Jackson, South Carolina. After deploying to Hawaii, it landed on Guam under IIIAC in July 1944 to fight under Marine command. It next fought on Leyte under Sixth Army from December 1944 through February 1945. Under the command of Major-General Andrew B. Bruce, the "Statue of Liberty Division" served as the Western Landing Force to first seize islands west of Okinawa.

The **81st Infantry Division**, under Major-General Paul J. Mueller, on New Caledonia was assigned as the Area Reserve and was not committed to Okinawa.

US MARINE CORPS

The Marine Corps' contribution to Tenth Army was **III Amphibious Corps**. IIIAC, so designated as it had previously served as the Third Fleet's landing force, had originated as I Marine Amphibious Corps (IMAC) on 1 October 1942 at San Diego, California. It initially served as an operational headquarters for most Marine forces in the South Pacific to control Marine operations on Guadalcanal, Russell Islands, New Georgia, and Bougainville into 1944. Besides Marine units, it had operational control of US Army and New Zealand units. On 15 April 1944, IMAC's support units were transferred to the new VAC Marine Administrative Command and IMAC's tactical elements were redesignated IIIAC on Guadalcanal. It was given the mission of seizing Guam in July followed by the Peleliu operation in September. IIIAC returned to Guadalcanal to prepare for the Okinawa Gunto assault under Major-General Roy S. Geiger.

III Amphibious Corps Artillery, under Brigadier-General David R. Nimmer, consisted of two three-battalion provisional groups to support the Corps' two divisions. Other IIIAC units included a provisional AAA group with four battalions, an engineer group with a four-battalion naval construction regiment and one Army and one Marine engineer battalion, and a service group built around the 7th Field Depot. The Corps' non-divisional troops totaled over 12,000.

Only two Marine divisions were to fight on Okinawa, although a third was to play an important role. Unlike Army divisions, the Marine divisions deployed with 100 per cent infantry strength plus 2,500 replacements (initially used as a shore party). The Marine Corps' efficient Replacement and Training Command was responsible for this. The Marine Corps, with only six divisions, was able to funnel replacements to IIIAC's divisions while they recovered from their last operation and prepared for the next. Their replacements had already been absorbed before the other three divisions were committed to Iwo Jima under VAC. Now those divisions were being rebuilt for the invasion of Japan. Each assault division was reinforced with a naval construction[13], an armored amphibian tractor, and two amphibian tractor battalions, plus numerous smaller Marine and Army support units.

The **1st Marine Division**, the "Old Breed," was formed from the 1st Marine Brigade at Guantánamo Bay, Cuba, on 1 February 1941 (the 1st

F4U Corsair fighters of four Marine Aircraft Group 31 (MAG-31) fighting squadrons were operating from Yontan Airfield after 7 April, providing close air support and combat air patrols. This was the first air unit to arrive on the island. Conditions were crude, requiring the fighters' 234-gal. (1,064-litre) fuel tanks be filled from 5-gal. (23-litres) cans. (US Army)

Brigade was organized in 1935). It was the first US division committed to combat when it landed on Guadalcanal in August 1942. It fought on New Britain from December 1943 and into 1944, and then assaulted Peleliu in August. There it experienced the first Japanese cave defenses, making it the division best prepared for Okinawa. It staged on Pavuvu for the Okinawa assault under Major-General Pedro A. del Valle with over 26,000 troops.

The **6th Marine Division** was the newest in the Corps, but seven of its nine infantry battalions were combat experienced. The 1st Provisional Marine Brigade was formed from separate units on 19 April 1944 on Guadalcanal and fought on Guam in July. The 6th Mar. Div. was activated on 7 September 1944 at Tassafaronga, Guadalcanal using the Brigade as a core with the 4th and 22nd Marines. The 4th Marines, made up of the former raider battalions (Midway, Guadalcanal, Makin, Pavuvu, New Georgia, Bougainville), had secured Emirau and fought on Guam. The 22nd Marines had fought on Eniwetok and Guam and secured islands in the Marshalls. The then separate 1st Battalion, 29th Marines had fought on Saipan and Tinian. These units were joined by the remainder of the 29th Marines, activated in the States. The Division's more than 24,000 troops were commanded by Major-General Lemuel C. Shepherd, Jr.

The **2nd Marine Division** was formed from the 2nd Marine Brigade on 1 February 1941 at San Diego (the 2nd Brigade was formed there in 1936 and later served in China). Most of the division fought on Guadalcanal in 1942–43. Its next fight was the brutal Betio Island assault in Tarawa Atoll in November 1943. It then fought on Saipan and Tinian in the summer of 1944. The 22,000-man division, under Major-General Thomas E. Watson, served as the demonstration force off Okinawa and then as a floating reserve. It soon departed for Saipan to serve as an area reserve. Its 8th Marines Special Landing Force returned to secure offshore islands in June and then came ashore to be attached to the 1st Marine Division for the rest of the campaign.

US TACTICAL ORGANIZATION

On the surface US Army and Marine divisions appear to have been organized similarly, but there were many internal differences in structure, manning, weapons, and equipment. It would be wrong to suggest the structure of either was superior. Both Army and Marine divisions conducted extensive amphibious operations and fought the same enemy on the same terrain, and both demonstrated strengths and weaknesses. Marine divisions may have been designed specifically for amphibious assault, but Army divisions, even though more heavily equipped and lavishly supplied with motor transport, were easily tailored for the mission. In 1945 Army divisions were smaller than Marine divisions; some 14,000 troops as opposed to 19,000 in the Marines, but were more heavily armed in many categories of weapons. The Army reinforced its divisions with support units to 22,000 troops and the Marines up to 26,000 (including attached replacements). Organic and attached units for both services' divisions are listed in the Order of Battle tables (see pages 90–93).

It should be noted that while both divisions had four howitzer battalions, the Army had three 105-mm and one 155-mm while the Marines had four 105-mm (except 1/11, 1st Mar. Div., which still had 75-mm pack howitzers). Marine divisions had a rocket detachment with 12 truck-mounted 4.5-in. Mk 7 launchers. The Army employed a 4.5-in. rocket battalion. A total of 35 American artillery battalions fought on Okinawa. Army and Marine artillery battalions had three batteries of four howitzers regardless of caliber.

Army and Marine infantry regiments differed greatly, although they used much the same weaponry. Both had three battalions, each with three rifle companies of three rifle platoons of three rifle squads – there the similarity ends. Army regimental strength was 3,068, but those on Okinawa began about 300 men under strength[14]. They were task organized for combat into regimental combat teams (RCT) by attaching engineer combat and medical collecting companies, and special troops detachments. The regimental cannon company had six 105-mm M7 self-propelled howitzers, excellent assault guns to blast caves and pillboxes, and the antitank company had nine 37-mm M3A1 guns. The 860-man infantry battalions had a headquarters company and a heavy weapons company with eight .30cal. M1917A1 water-cooled machine guns and six 81mm M1 mortars. The three 193-man rifle companies had three 39-man rifle platoons with three 12-man squads, each with a Browning automatic rifle (M1918A2 BAR), 11 M1 rifles, and one M7 rifle grenade launcher. The weapons platoon had two .30cal. M1919A4 air-cooled machine guns and three 60mm M2 mortars. Several 2.36in. M9 rocket launchers (bazookas) and M2-2 flamethrowers were available.

Companies were lettered in sequence through the regiment: 1st Bn – A–D, 2nd Bn – E–H, and 3rd Bn – I–M (no J); D, H, and M were heavy weapons. There were also regimental headquarters (with a reconnaissance and intelligence platoon) and service companies. Regimental companies (HQ, Service, Cannon, AT) were unlettered.

While the Army infantry regiment had changed little during the war, the Marine regiment[15] had evolved considerably. The divisions were still ostensibly organized under the May 1944 tables, but the 3,400-man regiments destined for Okinawa were organized under the 1 May 1945 tables, which were implemented earlier in the year. The 996-man infantry battalion no longer had a separate weapons company (they were disbanded and the weapons reassigned to the units that habitually used them). The battalion headquarters company's mortar platoon had four 81-mm mortars. The company also had a 55-man assault platoon with three assault sections (two seven-man squads with a flamethrower, a 2.36-in. bazooka, and demolition men) to support each rifle company. The 242-man rifle company had a 51-man headquarters with a section of three 60-mm mortars while the 46-man machine gun platoon had eight .30cal. air-cooled and six .30cal. water-cooled machine guns. The 45-man rifle platoons had three 13-man squads: squad leader (M1 carbine) and three fire teams each with team leader (M1 rifle, M7 grenade launcher), rifleman (M1 rifle, M7 GL), automatic rifleman (BAR), and assistant automatic rifleman (M1 rifle, M7 GL)[16]. The regimental weapons company had two antitank platoons with four 37-mm guns each and a platoon of four 105-mm M7 self-propelled howitzers. The regimental headquarters and service company included a 43-man scout and sniper platoon.

Marine companies were lettered the same as in Army regiments, but there were no D, H, and M weapons companies (companies were not re-lettered after the reorganization, except in the new 29th Marines where they were lettered in sequence). Marine infantry regiments were task organized into combat teams (CT) by attaching engineer, pioneer (shore party), motor transport, and medical companies, plus smaller service elements.

Army medium tank battalions had 17 M4A3 Shermans (75-mm gun) in each of their three companies and three in the headquarters. Marine tank battalions had 15 M4A2s (1st Battalion) or M4A3s (6th Battalion) in their three companies plus one more in the headquarters. The Army employed the M4A1-equipped 713th Tank Battalion (Armored Flamethrower), the first of its kind; its Company B supported the Marines. Army companies had three five-tank platoons, while the Marines used four three-tank platoons; both companies had two tanks in the headquarters. The seven tank battalions on Okinawa would lose 153 tanks (51 were Marine) to mines, antitank guns, artillery, and suicide squads – in that order.

The six Army and five Marine amphibian tractor battalions had three companies with about 30 LVT(3) or LVT(4) Amtracs each. The three Army amphibian tank, and two Marine armored amphibian tractor battalions each had four companies with 18 LVT(A)(4) 75-mm howitzer-armed amphibian tanks each. These were used as self-propelled artillery once ashore.

To control land-based aircraft supporting the campaign, a joint air command was organized in the form of **Tactical Air Force, Tenth Army** (TG 99.2). TAF was activated on 21 November 1944 at Schofield Barracks, Hawaii. The 2nd Marine Aircraft Wing (2nd MAW) doubled as Headquarters, TAF under Major-General Francis P. Mulcahy, who was relieved due to poor health by Louis E. Woods on 11 June 1945.

Initial close air support (CAS) for troops ashore was provided by Marine and Navy units aboard TF 51 escort carriers, but as airfields were seized and repaired, TAF units staged ashore to assume increasing CAS responsibilities. Besides CAS, TAF was also responsible for photo reconnaissance, resupply drops to front-line troops, and offensive air missions against *Kamikazes* and conventional air raids to protect the fleet and troops ashore. Besides TAF's CAS aircraft, Navy aircraft from TFs 51 and 58 also provided CAS. TAF, along with TF 58, attacked enemy airfields in the northern Ryukyus and Japan to stifle increasing air raids. On 1 July 1945, TAF, Tenth Army was redesignated TAF, Ryukyus. TAF was dissolved on 14 July 1945.

TAF was composed of four Marine aircraft groups with 15 fighting squadrons (three with night fighters), two Marine torpedo-bombing squadrons, plus three US Army Air Force (USAAF) fighter groups with ten fighter squadrons, two heavy (B-24), one medium (B-25), and one light (A-26) bombardment groups to eventually total over 750 aircraft. Marine landing force air support control units accompanied Army and Marine units ashore to direct CAS.

IMPERIAL JAPANESE FORCES

Prior to the neutralization of Truk in early 1944 Okinawa Gunto was lightly defended by the battalion-size *Nakagusuku Wan* Fortress Artillery Unit and a few guard companies. To bolster the island's defenses, the Japanese **32nd Army** was organized on 1 April 1944, one year to the day before the Americans landed. The first combat unit to arrive was the veteran 17,000-man 9th Division[17] from Manchuria in June 1944 while Saipan was under attack. In late June, a mere 600 survivors of the 44th Independent Mixed Brigade (IMB) arrived. US submarines had attacked its convoy sending 5,000 troops to the bottom. The 15th Independent

Mixed Regiment was flown in during July, Japan's first attempt to airlift such a large force, followed by the 24th Division shipped from Manchuria. The 62nd Division arrived in August from China.

The Imperial Japanese Army (IJA) was organized into army groups (named major regional command with two or more area armies), area armies (named or numbered area command with two or more armies and an air army), armies (corps-size with two or more divisions, one or more IMBs, and numerous army support troops; there were no formations designated corps), divisions, and independent mixed brigades (IMB).

The infantry regiment was the main tactical maneuver unit. Support troops for armies and divisions consisted of numerous independent battalions, units, and companies. The nondescript term "unit" is frequently encountered. A unit could range in size from a small platoon to a battalion or larger size support unit. The internal structure of infantry and artillery regiments was not unlike US practices with three battalions. However, certain combat and support "regiments" (tank, reconnaissance, engineer, transport) were battalion-size consisting of three to five companies with no battalion structure. Companies and batteries were numbered in sequence within regiments and independent battalions. Construction and pioneer units were manned mainly by Koreans and to a lesser degree by impressed labor from other occupied areas (Formosa, Okinawa, Manchuria).

IJA infantry divisions (*Shidan*) were found organized into one of two very different structures: the traditional three-infantry regiment "triangular division" and the "brigaded division", which appeared early in the war in an effort to conserve manpower but retain firepower. Supporting units were streamlined and the infantry were concentrated into two brigades. Both types of division relied largely on army-level units for service support.

The **62nd Division**, under the command of Lieutenant-General Takeo Fujioka, was activated in June 1943 in Shansi Province, China

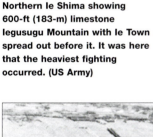

Northern Ie Shima showing 600-ft (183-m) limestone Iegusugu Mountain with Ie Town spread out before it. It was here that the heaviest fighting occurred. (US Army)

from the 4th and 6th IMBs, themselves formed in 1938. Both brigades and the Division had fought in China. The 62nd was a "brigaded division" comprising the 63rd and 64th Infantry Brigades. Both arrived with four 1,080-man independent infantry battalions (IIB), each with a machine gun company, an infantry gun company, and five rifle companies. In January both brigades received an additional 683-man IIB, but with only a machine gun company and three rifle companies and a platoon-size gun unit. Roughly 300-man engineer, signal, and transport units completed the 62nd Division along with a field hospital. It had no organic artillery.

With the withdrawal of the 9th Division in December, the strongest formation on Okinawa was the **24th Division** under Lieutenant-General Tatsumi Amamiya. Raised in Manchuria in December 1939, it had seen no combat, but was well trained. It was a "triangular division" with the roughly 2,800-man 22nd, 32nd, and 89th infantry regiments. Each had three battalions and a regimental gun company. The battalions had one machine gun, antitank, and infantry gun company each (the 3rd Battalions had an 81-mm mortar platoon in lieu of the gun company), and three rifle companies. The 42nd Artillery Regiment had three battalions, the 1st and 2nd with one 75-mm gun and two 100-mm howitzer batteries. The 3rd Battalion had three 150-mm howitzer batteries (Japanese batteries had four pieces). The 24th Reconnaissance Regiment had a machine gun and two rifle companies, 24th Engineer Regiment had three companies and the 24th Transport Regiment had five (three motor and two horse). There were also 200–300-man signal, water supply, and medical units.

The battered **44th Independent Mixed Brigade** had to be completely rebuilt on Okinawa and Kyushu, but it never achieved full strength and some elements were detached to Okinawa's north end. Under the command of Major-General Suzuki Shigeki, it had been organized on Kyushu for service on Okinawa. Its regimental-sized 2nd Infantry Unit was rebuilt, unlike the 1st, which was replaced by the 15th Independent Mixed Regiment (IMR). Both the 2nd Unit and 15th IMR were organized the same, with three battalions and regimental gun and antitank companies. The 700-man battalions had one machine-gun company and three rifle companies and a gun unit. Brigade units included a two-battery 75-mm howitzer unit, signal unit, and an engineer company. Most of the 2nd Unit – 1st and 2nd Battalions, gun and antitank companies – was detached to form the "*Udo* Force" (also known as "*Kunigami* Detachment") for service in the north.

While infantry regiments and battalions were of varied organization and strength, there were similarities. Regimental gun companies usually had four 75-mm Model 41 infantry guns and regimental and battalion antitank companies had 4–6 x 37-mm Model 94 "antitank" guns (actually rapid-fire infantry support guns). Battalion machine gun companies had eight or 12 x 7.7-mm Model 92 tripod-mounted heavy machine guns. Battalion gun companies had four 70-mm Model 92 infantry guns (sometimes substituted by 81-mm Model 97 mortars) while "gun units" had only two. Rifle companies varied widely; at full-strength they usually had three rifle platoons with three 13–15-man light machine sections (actually rifle squads with a Model 11, 96, or 99 bipod-mounted machine gun and one or two 50-mm Model 89 grenade dischargers – "knee mortars") and a 13–15-man grenade discharger section with three more "knee mortars" and more riflemen. Larger battalions' rifle companies often had a weapons' platoon with two heavy machine guns and two 20-mm Model 97 antitank rifles.

Non-divisional artillery units were under the **5th Artillery Group** to include Imperial Japanese Navy (IJN) coast defense gun companies. Major-General Kosuke Wada controlled the equivalent of nine IJA artillery battalions with 36 x 150-mm howitzers, 8 x 150-mm guns, 8 x 240-mm howitzers, 24 x 320-mm spigot mortars, and 96 x 81-mm mortars. Additionally, the artillery units of the 24th Division and 44th IMB were attached to the Group. The **21st Antiaircraft Artillery Group** fielded four AAA battalions with 72 x 75-mm AA guns and three machine cannon battalions with 54 x 20-mm cannons total. The two shipping engineer regiments of the **11th Shipping Group** operated IJA landing craft and later served as an ill-fated seaborne raiding force. The battalion-size **27th Tank Regiment** contained the 32nd Army's armor in the form of 13 Model 95 (1935) *Ha-Go* 37-mm light tanks and 14 Model 97 (1937) *Chi-Ha* 57-mm medium tanks plus a rifle company. There were also three independent antitank battalions with 18 excellent 47-mm Model 1 guns each and four independent [heavy] machine gun battalions.

Significant service, support, engineer, and signal units were under the control of either the 32nd Army or the 49th Line of Communications Sector. Airfield and aircraft service units were subordinate to the 19th Air Sector Command.

In June 1944, the IGHQ authorized the establishment of a Labor Unit (*Boeitai*) in the 20–50 age group. About 16,600 Okinawans augmented regular units (100 per battalion); others formed the "Blood and Iron for the Emperor" Duty Unit (*Tekketsu Kinnotai*) and special guard engineer units, while most simply reinforced the labor troops and were unarmed. Up to 39,000 *Boeitai* were conscripted. There were other organizations such as the Civil Defense Unit (*Keibotai*), organized in each town in February 1945 to fight air raid fires and maintain order, and the Home Defense Unit (*Keibitai*), raised in October 1944 with lightly armed 65-man self-defense platoons. A further manpower pool was tapped on 1 January 1945 when 32nd Army directed that all fit male islanders between the ages of 17 and 45 could be mobilized to augment the *Boeitai* laborers. This included thousands more on other Nansei

Shoto islands. Unknown thousands were conscripted[18]. Okinawans had no warrior tradition and they frustrated the Japanese with their indifference to military service. Some 600 middle school girls were trained as nurses.

IJA troops numbered 67,000. About 5,000 were Okinawan conscripts assigned to regular Japanese units. Over 12,000 Korean laborers and comfort women were present.

About 29,000 32nd Army troops belonged to labor, service, and specialized support units. In March, 18,500 service troops were reorganized into ad hoc "specially established" rifle units. These units' strength are not included in the listed strength of the divisions and 44th IMB to which they were attached. The 11th Shipping Group formed the 1st Specially Established Brigade with the 2nd–4th Specially Established Regiments and attached to the 24th Division. Ground service units of the 49th Line of Communications Sector were organized into the 2nd Specially Established Brigade with the 5th and 6th Specially Established Regiments and attached to the 62nd Division. The 6th was reattached to the 44th IMB in late May. The 1st Especially Established Regiment was raised by the 19th Air Sector Command and also attached to the 62nd to defend Yontan and Kadena Airfields. The 1st–3rd and 26th Independent battalions were formed from like-numbered IJA sea raiding base battalions in February. They were attached to the 24th and 62nd Divisions, and 44th IMB. A final ad hoc unit was the 50th Specially Established Battalion on Ie Shima. These units were armed only with rifles, hand grenades, and a few "knee mortars" and light machine guns. They were employed to screen flanks, man secondary lines, and eventually were fed into regular units as replacements. The Japanese often astounded the American command by their ability to reconstitute battered units from survivors and ad hoc replacements to include the use of captured weapons.

Some 3,825 **Imperial Japanese Navy** personnel and over 6,000 civilian combatant employees were assigned to the Okinawa Naval Base Force's 15 coast defense companies (120-mm and 140-mm guns), four antiaircraft company groups (20 x 120-mm, 77 x 25-mm, 60 x 13.2-mm AA); Oroku Detachment, 951st Air Group, Nansei Shoto Air Group; 226th and 3210th Construction Units, a mortar battery (18 x 81-mm), and naval base service personnel. Other units included the 27th Torpedo Boat, 33rd Midget Submarine, and 37th Torpedo Maintenance Units. The Base Force was formed in April 1944 and was under the command of Rear-Admiral Teiso Nippa. It defended the Oroku Peninsula and was headquartered at Tomigusuki south of Naha. Most IJN air group, construction, and service personnel, who included Okinawan conscripts and Korean laborers, were reorganized into several small untrained "naval attack force" rifle battalions. Additionally, some 1,100 *Boeitai* were assigned to the IJN.

---

13 Naval construction battalions were commonly known as "Seabees" due to their "CB" initials.

14 The subordinate unit strengths given are the authorized full strength.

15 Marine regiments did not bear functional designations, but were referred to simply as, for example, 4th Marines. Thus on Okinawa the 1st, 4th, 5th, 7th, 8th, 22nd, and 29th Marines were infantry and the 10th, 11th, and 15th Marines were artillery.

16 The fire team concept evolved from the Banana Wars in the 1920s and 1930s. The team was built around an automatic weapon and proved very successful.

17 The 9th Division was organized in 1895 and fought in the 1904–05 Russo-Japanese War and in China from 1937 to 1939. It consisted of the 7th, 19th, and 35th Infantry and 9th Mountain Artillery Regiments.

18 It is unclear what the organization and relationship of these units was. Most post-war writers refer to them collectively only as the *Boeitai*.

INITIAL OPERATIONS

PRELIMINARY STRIKES

The war first reached Okinawa Gunto on 29 September 1944 when B-29s bombed the airfields. This raid's main purpose was to photograph as much of Okinawa and its outlying islands as possible. The first raid by carrier aircraft followed on 10 October, an operation intended to neutralize the air threat to the approaching Leyte invasion force. The Japanese referred to this action as the Air Battle of Formosa. The Japanese lost 500 aircraft and 36 ships in three days. Okinawa was granted a respite until the new year brought a massive carrier raid on 3 January. The Fast Carrier Force (TF 38) returned on 10 January for an even more punishing raid. The January operations were in conjunction with raids on Formosa and the China coast. The Fast Carrier Force (now designated TF 58) struck targets in the Tokyo area through late February. While retiring to Ulithi, TF 58 struck Okinawa on 1 March with an extremely vicious raid.

American submarines and patrol bombers effectively isolated the Ryukyus from Japan and Formosa, sinking scores of cargo ships. Between attacks on Japan, B-29s conducted numerous attacks on Okinawa. By the end of March there were almost no operational Japanese aircraft in the Ryukyus. Naha City and its port were completely destroyed as was Shuri and its ancient treasures. Between 18 and 31 March, TF 58 conducted further strikes on Kyushu airfields and

Looking south from Hill 178 in the 7th Inf. Div. zone near Okinawa's east coast. It was from the far ridge that the Japanese 89th Infantry, 24th Division had launched its futile 4 May counteroffensive. The 7th Inf. Div. soon seized the ridgeline as it fought through the Shuri outer defenses. (US Army)

Marines in a water-filled 60-mm M2 mortar pit, 5 May. Its leather combination M4 muzzle cap and carrying sling are in place to keep rain out of the barrel. Adjacent to the pit a poncho has been staked out to provide some degree of shelter from the heavy rains. The gunner to the left carries a Mk 2 "K-Bar" fighting and utility knife. The term "K-Bar" is the firm's name and was derived from the endorsement of a satisfied pre-war customer who stated he had "killed a bar" (bear) with one of their knives, with the result that the company adopted the new name. (USMC)

An Army rifle squad checks out a tomb strongpoint it has just destroyed with large satchel charges, 7 May. The force of the explosion shattered the entrance and blew the defenders through the opening. (US Army)

Japanese warships in preparation for *Iceberg*. The Japanese counter-attacked the carriers, almost sinking the USS *Franklin* (CV-13), but failed to inflict serious damage on the task force. On 24 March, the force sank an entire eight-ship convoy northwest of Okinawa. On the same date, five 16-in. gun battleships and 11 destroyers shelled targets on Okinawa. Between 26 and 31 March, the British Carrier Force struck Sakishima Gunto to the southwest of Okinawa neutralizing its airfields.

The Japanese, expecting a landing on Okinawa or Formosa at any time, alerted its air forces for the *Ten-Go* Operation on 25 March. On 27 and 31 March, massive B-29 strikes on the Kyushu airfields effectively shut them down. The Japanese managed to launch only 50 two-aircraft attacks prior to L-Day damaging eight US ships. *Ten-Go* was not able to launch until 6 April, five days after the main landing.

Task Force 52's Mine Flotilla (TG 52.2) began sweeping the approaches to Okinawa on 22 March with 122 mine and patrol craft. By L-Day, 3,000 square miles of ocean were swept, resulting in the discovery of six minefields and the destruction of another 257 mines.

On 25 March, the Gunfire and Covering Force moved in with three 16-in., five 14-in., and one 12-in. gun battleships; seven 8-in. and three 6-in. gun cruisers, 32 destroyers and escorts, and 177 gunboats. Some 37,000 rounds of 5-in. and larger, 33,000 4.5-in. rockets, and 22,500 4.2-in. mortar rounds were fired in the seven days before L-Day. The Carrier Force delivered 3,100 strike sorties. They had little effect, although the few remaining Japanese aircraft on the island were destroyed. The Japanese had pulled back from the beaches to their underground shelters and refused to respond to attacks.

In the meantime, elements of the amphibious forces departed Leyte and Ulithi. They encountered rough weather en route with many groups barely making their target date.

INITIAL LANDINGS

Kerama Retto is a group of eight rugged islands (plus smaller islets) 15 miles (24 km) west of Okinawa. Unsuited for airfields, they were an ideal anchorage capable of accommodating over 70 large ships. The Keramas would become the fleet's refueling, rearming, and repair base. The proposal for its early capture was initially resisted because of the fear of air attack. The need for such a base was realized during the Iwo Jima assault. The Western Island Attack Group, 77th Inf. Div. embarked, swept through the Keramas from the west on 26 March (L-6). Five of the

Troops of the 305th Infantry, 77th Inf. Div. fire on attacking Japanese with M1 rifles during the approach to the Shuri Line, 11 May. Note that the two soldiers to the right carry .45cal. M1919A1 pistols, indicating they may be members of a weapons crew. Note the helmet marking in the shape of the division's patch on the man to the left. (US Army)

Division's infantry battalions (1/305, 3/305, 1/306, 2/306, 2/307) and two artillery battalions (304, 305 FA) secured the islands with little resistance by 29 May. Only four of the islands were defended by 975 IJN troops. Japanese losses were 530 dead and 121 prisoners. Some 1,200 civilians were interned, after almost 150 had committed suicide. Over 350 suicide boats were captured. American losses were 31 dead and 81 wounded. About 300 IJN troops remained unmolested on Tokashiki under a gentlemen's agreement until they surrendered after V-J Day. The 77th Inf. Div. re-embarked on 30 March leaving 2/305 behind for security. It was relieved by a provisional infantry battalion formed from the 870th Antiaircraft Artillery Battalion on 23 May. The floating fleet base and a seaplane base were in operation before the islands were fully secured. On 31 March, PB4Y Catalinas of Fleet Air Wing 1, operating from seaplane tenders, began anti-shipping patrols over the East China Sea, local anti-submarine patrols, and air-sea rescue support for carrier operations.

Keise Shima (actually four sand islets), 11 miles (18 km) southwest of the Hagushi Beaches, was secured unopposed by 2/306 Infantry early on 31 March. Marine scouts had previously confirmed the islets were unoccupied. The 420th Field Artillery Group came ashore with the 531st and 532nd FA Battalions to support the main landing and cover southern Okinawa with their 155-mm guns. The Japanese made several unsuccessful attempts to destroy the guns.

Underwater demolition teams (UDT) reconnoitered the Hagushi Beaches on 29 March. Spotter aircraft over Okinawa reported no human beings were visible. The entire island appeared deserted. At 1000hrs, 30 March, frogmen of UDTs 4, 7, 11, 16, 17, and 21 swam in to demolish anti-boat obstacles. The water temperature was a debilitating 70°F (21°C).

The amphibious force assembled just west of Okinawa. The Carrier Force took up station some 50 miles (80 km) to the east. On 31 March, the Demonstration Group, 2nd Mar. Div. embarked, arriving off the southeast Minatogawa Beaches, which the Japanese considered the most likely site for the main landing. This deception was reinforced by UDT scouts and minesweepers operating offshore since 29 March.

MAIN LANDING

Easter Sunday and April Fool's Day, 1 April 1945 – L-Day. Sunrise 0621hrs, temperature 74°F (23.3°C), 5–7 miles (8–11 km) visibility with smoke and haze, moderate east–northeast winds, sea conditions – light swell, no surf on the Hagushi Beaches, high tide (5 ft 11 in./1.79 km) at 0900hrs.

Over 1,300 TF 51, 52, 53, 54, and 55 ships were assembled off Okinawa. Transports and LSTs dropped anchor 3–7 miles (4.8–11 km) – offshore. Admiral Kelly Turner gave the order, "Land the landing force" at 0406hrs. Troops began to load their amphibian tractors and landing craft to launch at 0630hrs and circle awaiting the final signal.

At 0530hrs the pre-landing barrage smothered a zone 1,000 yds (914 m) inland with some 25 rounds per 100 sq yds (84 sq m). As the sun rose behind the hilly island, seasick soldiers and marines saw smoke-shrouded Okinawa Shima for the first time. At 0800hrs, dozens of

THE LANDING BEACHES, 1 APRIL 1945

Legend:
- 0 – 10 m
- 10 – 50 m
- 50 – 100 m
- 100 – 150 m
- above 150 m
- Japanese strongpoints
- US Marines
- US Army
- L-Day (evening of 1 April) positions

Zampo Misaki

Nagahama

1st SPECIALLY ESTABLISHED REGIMENT

Yontan Airfield

Irammiya

6 Mar
1 Mar

GREEN 1
GREEN 2
RED 1
RED 2
RED 3
BLUE 1
BLUE 2
YELLOW 1
YELLOW 2
PURPLE 1
PURPLE 2
ORANGE 1
ORANGE 2
WHITE
WHITE 2
WHITE 3
BROWN

Hagushi (Togushi)

Bishi

Bridge captured intact

Kadena Airfield

Sunabe

Momobaru

Chatan

Atanniya

Futema

2 | 22
1 | 22   3 | 22
6 Mar (-)
2 | 4
Div Res
3 | 4
1 | 4
III
3 | 7   1 | 7
1 Mar
29
Corps Res
3 | 5
Div Res
2 | 5
1 | 5
III
XXIV
3 | 17
2 | 17   1 | 17
7
3 | 32
2 | 32   1 | 32
184
Div Res
3 | 381
2 | 381
1 | 381
7
96
XXIV
382
Corps Res
96(-)
1 | 383   2 | 383
3 | 383

1 2 3 4

N

0   1 mile
0   1 km

55

LCI(G) gunboats cruised on line toward the beaches with 3-in. and 40-mm guns blazing. At 0815hrs hundreds of circling Amtracs formed into assault waves.

Control craft pennants came down five minutes later and an eight-mile line of churning Amtracs began their 4,000-yard (3,658-m) run to the beaches. Two groups of 64 carrier planes strafed and bombed the beaches as naval gunfire shifted inland. As four American divisions ran in toward the shore, the 2nd Mar. Div. at the Minatogawa Beaches executed its diversionary feint. Ironically, the first troop casualties were suffered by this force as *Kamikazes* crashed into a transport and LST. Other than attracting air attacks, the demonstration failed to draw Japanese reinforcements. The Japanese had no reason to send troops from the Hagushi Beaches; few were there and other units were positioned exactly where Ushijima wanted them.

The first wave soon passed the battleship USS *Tennessee* (BB-43), 2,000 yds (1,829-m) from the beaches, its 14-in. guns leveled and firing shattering broadsides into the sea walls. Most assault regimental landing

A 76-mm gun-armed M18 "Hellcat" tank destroyer of the Antitank Company, 306th Infantry, 77th Inf. Div. fires on the Shuri Line, 11 May. Atop the turret are .50cal. HB-M2 and .30cal. M1919A4 machine guns. Note the crew's haversacks in the turret bustle rack and the spare treads on the turret rear. (US Army)

A .30cal. M1917A1 water-cooled heavy machine gun provides covering fire for advancing marines on 11 May. This weapon could maintain accurate long-range supporting fire for prolonged periods. The ground is littered with discarded ammunition boxes, damaged weapons, and discarded equipment. (USMC)

teams, two battalions abreast, consisted of eight waves: 1st – 28 LVT(A)(4) amtanks firing 75-mm howitzers to "shoot ashore" the following waves; 2nd – 16 LVT(4) Amtracs with assault troops; 3rd through 6th – 12 LVT(4)s each with more assault troops and crew-served weapons; 7th – varied numbers of LSMs or LCMs with flotation device-equipped Sherman tanks; and 8th – LVT(4)s with support troops.

The LCI(G) gunboats halted outside the reef and the assault waves passed landing at 0830hrs – H-Hour. Only sporadic Japanese mortar and artillery fire fell. The sea walls were breached by naval gunfire at numerous points. Resistance ashore was virtually nil as the untrained 3,473 airfield service troops of the 1st Specially Established Regiment dissolved. Only half of the unit was armed and there were virtually no heavy weapons. Okinawa was not the feared repeat of Peleliu and Iwo Jima with troops slaughtered on the beaches. In the first hour 50,000 troops landed. Blasted suicide boats and small craft were found choking the Bishi Gawa separating IIIAC and XXIV Corps zones. As soldiers and marines pressed inland the Amtracs swarmed back to pick up reserve battalions. These were followed by LCVPs with regimental support troops and supplies. Larger landing craft and ships began delivering divisional artillery and support troops at 1400hrs. The receding tide exposed the reef and the unloading of heavy equipment slowed. Late morning found the 4th Marines on the edge of Yontan Airfield and the 17th Infantry at Kadena. The two airfields were not expected to be captured until L+3.

By nightfall a 15,000-yd (13,716-m) beachhead, 5,000 yds (4,572 m) deep in places, was firmly established and another 10,000 troops had landed. The units were deployed, left to right, 6th Mar. Div, 1st Mar. Div, 7th Inf. Div, and 96th Inf. Div. A 600-yd (549-m) gap existed between IIIAC and XXIV Corps, but this was closed the next day. The four assault divisions reported only 28 dead, 27 missing, and 104 wounded this first day on Okinawa Shima.

While ineffective in Europe, the little 37-mm M3A1 antitank gun still had value in the Pacific Theater. Its compact size and comparatively light weight allowed it to be manhandled into position over rough ground to engage pillboxes and caves with armor-piercing, high explosive, and canister rounds. The latter was useful for countering infantry attacks and stripping camouflaging foliage from enemy positions. It remained effective against Japanese tanks as well. Note that this crew has attached a scalloped section of sheet metal to the shield to distort its distinctive straight upper edge. (USMC)

SPLITTING THE ISLAND

On the morning of L+1 the 2nd Mar. Div. conducted another demonstration off the southeast beaches to no avail, other than allowing Ushijima to claim he had forced their withdrawal. The two airfields were securely in American hands as were the surrounding hills. The defenders failed to place demolitions on the airfields, and by the afternoon of L+1 Kadena was usable for emergency landings. Yontan was usable on L+2. The main bridge over the Bishi Gawa was captured intact and the defenders had destroyed few bridges over smaller streams. The question in every one's mind was, "Where is the enemy?"

The weather remained favorable for the next two days and the Americans continued their rapid advance. The 6th Mar. Div. moved north and by 4 April had secured the narrow Ishikawa Isthmus. The 1st Mar. and 7th Inf. Divisions reached the east coast on the afternoon of the 3rd and the Marines secured the Katchin Peninsula on the 5th. The 96th Inf. Div. wheeled to its right and began moving south as did elements of the 7th on the east coast. By L+3 they were established on a line across the Chatan Isthmus facing south. All units were in positions they had expected to reach after two weeks of hard fighting.

The supply build-up continued and more support units landed. Empty transports departed and each night the fleet dispersed, but some fell victim to increasing air attacks. Hundreds of civilians were rounded up and interrogated. Military government units took over responsibility for their care. The information gleaned was sketchy and conflicting, but a picture emerged of a general Japanese withdrawal to the south prior to L-Day.

The weather turned for the worse on 4 April. The sea conditions were such that unloading was sometimes suspended. Rain turned roads into quagmires. Entire new roads were built between rain periods and the weak native bridges were replaced by steel Bailey bridges. The west coast highway was redesignated "US 1." Marine fighting squadrons arrived at Yontan on 7 April and at Kadena two days later to provide close air support (CAS).

To fully protect Tenth Army's eastern flank, the Eastern Islands lying northeast of the Katchin Peninsula in the Chimu Wan had to be secured. This was accomplished from 6–11 April by 3/105 of the 27th Inf. Div. supported by Fleet Marine Force Pacific (FMFPac) Amphibious Recon Battalion, UDT 7, and Army amtrac units; the remainder of the 105th Infantry served as the floating reserve aboard Eastern Islands Attack and Fire Support Group (TG 51.19). Most of the islands were unoccupied, except for Tsugen Shima, which was defended by Japanese 1st Battery, 7th Heavy Artillery Regiment. The battery lost 243 men and no prisoners were taken, but 30 escaped. US losses were 14 dead.

The American command could only guess at Japanese intentions. Air reconnaissance revealed nothing in the south (the Japanese remained underground). Some thought the enemy may have evacuated to other

RIGHT **The Japanese had blown this stone bridge over the Asato River, but American engineers quickly erected a steel Bailey bridge replacement on 14 May. It was better able to support heavy use by American vehicles than the stone bridge. (USMC)**

BELOW **A platoon of Marine 75-mm howitzer-armed landing vehicles, tracked (armored) Mk 4 (LVT[A]4) provide fire support. After landing armored amphibian tractor battalions were often attached to divisional artillery regiments to augment their indirect fire. Thought of as tanks by some, they were inferior to genuine tanks due to their high silhouette, thin armor, and poorer cross-country performance. (USMC)**

A rifle platoon of 2nd Battalion, 306th Infantry, 77th Inf. Div. atop the crest of a ridge searches for a sniper firing on them, 14 May. The soldier in the foreground is armed with a .30cal. M1918A2 Browning automatic rifle, around which a rifle squad built its base of fire. Note that many of the troops have dabbed light-colored mud on their dark olive drab helmets for camouflage. (US Army)

islands, or had been drawn to the southeast by the demonstrations, or were waiting to counterattack; that opportunity came and passed. Still, there was little response from the enemy.

The impact of the invasion was initially more devastating in the Home Islands than to Japanese forces on Okinawa. On 3 April, news of the landing was released. This was Emperor Jimmu Day, who 2,500 years earlier, had launched the conquest of Yamato (after which the battleship was named) to "make the universe our home." Premier Kuniaki Koiso claimed the Americans would be driven from Okinawa and Saipan recaptured. He was forced to resign the next day. Admiral (Baron) Kantaro Suzuki was appointed by the Emperor on 7 April to find an honorable way for Japan to end the war.

THE OFFENSIVE CONTINUES

TENTH ARMY ADVANCES

On 4 April General Hodge ordered the 7th and 96th Inf. divisions to attack south. The Japanese plan was to use the 62nd Division to hold the main northern defense line while the 24th Division and 44th IMB were held in reserve to destroy any new American landings on the southern coasts. The 62nd Division and its supporting artillery were in excellent positions on commanding terrain and had clear line of sight right across XXIV Corps' area on the plain below with its sparse vegetation. The artillery could fire on the Hagushi Beaches and Nakagusuku Wan. The 62nd Division's defense was echeloned with its 63rd Brigade dug-in across the island and the 64th defending the west coast on its flank.

Punching through the outposts, the two American divisions cautiously pushed south, meeting strong resistance on Cactus, Kaniku, and Tombstone Ridges[19]. A crag called "the Pinnacle" was captured on 6 April by the 184th Infantry after a tough fight. It was thought to be the point on which Commodore Perry raised the American flag in 1853. The 63rd Brigade put up a stiff enough resistance to halt XXIV Corps elements from 6–8 April. The covering force had held the Americans off for eight days inflicting over 1,500 casualties on the Corps but at a cost of almost 4,500 dead. The outer Shuri defenses were now uncovered and the Corps would continue its advance against even tougher resistance.

The 1,000-yd (914 m) long Kakazu Ridge stretched northwest to southeast on the northeast side of Kakazu Village. The reinforced 63rd

A 105mm M7 self-propelled howitzer is directed forward by marines on 24 May. The M7 proved to be an excellent assault weapon for direct fire against pillboxes and cave positions. Spare track sections are fastened to its sides for additional protection from antitank guns. The man in the foreground carries an SCR-300 "walkie-talkie" radio, the standard company-level radio. (US Army)

REDUCING A TOMB STRONGHOLD
The hillsides of southern Okinawa were dotted with tens of thousands of lyre-shaped tombs unique to the Okinawan culture. Generations of ancestors were buried in the limestone and concrete tombs. When a relative died the tomb was opened and the body interned in a front chamber to decompose. The bones were later cleaned and placed in ceramic urns in the tomb's main room. Families would have celebrations within the small wall-enclosed lawn fronting the tomb to honor their ancestors. The Japanese frequently converted the tombs to pillboxes by smashing in the small sealed entrance and emplacing a machine gun. The machine gun was supported by riflemen, and although the position lacked all-round fire, the flanks were protected by fire from other tombs and dug-in covering positions. There was, of course, no escape and they became tombs for Japanese soldiers as well. Thousands were destroyed along with the remains of many generations of ancestors. Many were blasted with artillery and tank fire merely on the suspicion that they might harbor Japanese defenders. The desecration of the tombs was a terrible affront to Okinawans. The reduction of a tomb required special tactics. An entire platoon might be required to reduce a fortified tomb and the adjacent covering positions. Artillery and mortars first saturated the tomb and surrounding area to kill any enemy on the surface and drive those within the defences away from firing positions. Under the cover of direct fire from tanks and self-propelled 105 mm howitzers the infantry would close in on the position's flanks staying out of the field of fire. Machine gun, BAR, rifle, and rifle grenade fire was directed at the firing port to cover bazooka, flamethrower, and demolition teams closing in from the flanks. The American's called this the "blowtorch and corkscrew," the Japanese called it "straddle tactics." (Howard Gerrard)

Brigade still manned the entire front. The 383rd Infantry, 96th Inf. Div. attacked the low hill mass on 9 April and was repulsed. After repeated attacks it was not until 12 April that the ridge was taken. The Japanese 63rd Brigade lost 5,750 men, the US 96th Division lost 451. During the Kakazu battles the 7th Inf. Div. to the east had made slow progress in rugged terrain against stiff resistance. The 7th Division's sector was only one-third of XXIV Corps' front, but the terrain forced narrow frontages and the almost nonexistent road system severely hampered logistics.

The 2nd Mar. Div, the Tenth Army Floating Reserve, departed for Saipan on 11 April. It was scheduled to land on Kikai, off Amami O Shima, northeast of Okinawa in July, but this landing never took place.

Chafing at their defensive strategy, the more aggressive Japanese officers clamored for a counterattack. Colonel Yahara held them at bay reasoning that even if a counterattack was successful, the troops would be exposed to massive American firepower on the plains. General Ushijima gave in when the Americans became stalled in the outer Shuri defenses. With difficulty the Japanese 22nd Infantry, 24th Division was moved north from the Oroku Peninsula to attack through the 63rd Brigade's line near the east coast. Elements of the 63rd Brigade would attack in the west along with the 272nd Independent Infantry Battalion (IIB), the 62nd Division reserve moved from Shuri.

The counterattack was launched at 1900hrs, 12 April with a 30-minute barrage to cover the infiltration. The attack was far too weak and uncoordinated as many commanders, realizing its folly, held back their troops. The 22nd Infantry, unfamiliar with the rugged terrain in front of the US 7th Inf. Div, foundered. The US 96th Inf. Div. faced a well-organized and sustained attack. The Japanese 272nd IIB's attack was well conducted and gave the US 381st Infantry a difficult night on Kakazu Ridge. The battle lasted into the night of 13/14 April. By dawn on the 14th it was all over. It delayed the American push a couple of days, but the Japanese lost hundreds of men and the Americans less than 100. The Americans continued to inch south and then prepared to assault the main Shuri defenses on even more rugged terrain. On 13 April President Franklin D. Roosevelt passed away, stunning most US personnel.

THE PUSH NORTH

While XXIV Corps fought slowly toward Shuri, IIIAC was engaged in a different kind of war. The 1st Mar. Div. defended Yontan Airfield, the landing beaches, and secured the zone behind XXIV Corps across the island. The 6th Mar. Div. had secured the Ishikawa Isthmus with the 22nd Marines to the north where the isthmus began to widen. On the morning of 6 April the 29th Marines launched a tank-supported push up the west coast while the 4th Marines moved up the east. Roads in the north were very limited and the terrain rugged with dense vegetation. Fire support was provided by the 2nd Field Artillery Group and 1st Armored Amphibian Tractor Battalion.

The Japanese had blown bridges and laid mines, but resistance was very light. Finally, on 8 April, after combing the hills, it was determined the enemy had concentrated on the Motobu Peninsula on the island's upper west coast. The 29th Marines now moved across the base of the

An 81-mm M1 mortar crew of 3rd Battalion, 22nd Marines, 6th Mar. Div. provides fire support. They are firing heavy high explosive rounds. These had a shorter range than the light HE, but their effect was equivalent to that of a 105-mm howitzer. (USMC)

An Army tank company prepares to advance from behind a ridge line. These M4A3 Shermans have had their large white stars painted over in black to prevent them from being used as aim points for antitank guns. The Japanese 47-mm Model 1 (1941) antitank gun, while of moderate performance when compared to similar contemporary weapons, was effective against Shermans. (US Army)

peninsula and westward. The 4th and 22nd Marines patrolled north and protected the 29th Marines' rear. Contacts increased over the next few days, but no decisive engagements were fought. Enemy resistance, exacerbated by worsening terrain, increased as the Marines moved west.

The enemy was positioned in a 6 x 8-mile (9.6 x 13-km) redoubt around the 1,200-ft (366-m) high Yae Take (Mount). The broken ground precluded the use of armor and was ideal for the defenders, the heavily armed 1,500-man "Udo Force" detached from the 44th IMB. Initial skirmishing and maneuvering lasted for days, but on 14 April the attack was begun in earnest by the 29th and 4th Marines. Numerous hills and ridges had to be taken during the approach to Yae Take. The 17th saw the final assault on the Take, but it was not cleared until the next day. Some 700 Japanese dead were counted; although enough managed to escape to conduct a lengthy guerrilla war in the wild north.

The guerrilla war was fought in countless small skirmishes, hit-and-run attacks, and sniping. To make matters worse, due to an effective propaganda effort many Okinawan irregulars fought with the Japanese and committed sabotage. Okinawan veterans with experience in China trained their fellows as home defense units. The 7th Marines, securing the Ishikawa Isthmus, was drawn into the guerrilla war as Japanese troops attempted to evade to the south.

On 4 May, the understrength 27th Inf. Div. relieved the 6th Mar. Div. in the north. The 6th had lost 236 dead and 1,601 wounded. Subordinate to the Island Command, the 27th Inf. Div. swept north fighting a ten-day battle on the 1,000-ft (305-m) Onna Take in late May and early June. On 4 August, the north was finally declared secure, although small pockets remained. Over 1,000 Japanese had been killed and some 500 prisoners taken.

IE SHIMA LANDINGS

Ie Shima (infrequently called Ie Jima) was codenamed *Indispensable.* It lies 3½ miles (5.6 km) off the west end of the Motobu Peninsula and 20 miles (32 km) north of the Hagushi Beaches. It is located at 26°43' N 127°47' E. The oval-shaped island is 5½ miles (9 km) long from east to west and 2¾ miles (4–5 km) wide. The north and northwest coasts are faced with cliffs up to 100 ft (30 m) high pockmarked with hundreds of caves. The south coast is lined with beaches which range in width from 9–35 yds (8–32 m) and are broken into sections of between 125 and 900 yds (114–823 m) long separated by low cliffs and outcroppings. The ground slopes gently inland from the beaches. The southwest coast and parts of the south are backed by bluffs. The entire island is surrounded by a coral reef several hundred yards wide, but it was not a major obstacle. Inland the ground rises to a level plateau averaging 165 ft (50.3 m) above sea level. Most of the island was served by a

Limit of US advance 16th April
Limit of US advance 17th April
Limit of US advance 18th April
Limit of US advance 19th April
Limit of US advance 20th April
Japanese strongpoint lines

Secured Minna 12–13 Apr

Landed 15 Apr

Mar Amph Recon

305
306
902

Minna Shima (4 miles)

307

305

Ie Town

307

Iegusugu Pinnacle (185 m)

306

306

Igawa Unit

Agarii-Mae Village

307

Bloody Ridge

306

305

RED T-4

306

307

RED T-3

307(-)

706(-)

305

2

Government House

307

17 Apr

306

305

305

305

K

306

305

RED T-2

305

306(-)

305

RED T-1

305

306

P A T R O L S

GREEN T-1

306

77(-)

304

N

1 mile

1 km

0

0

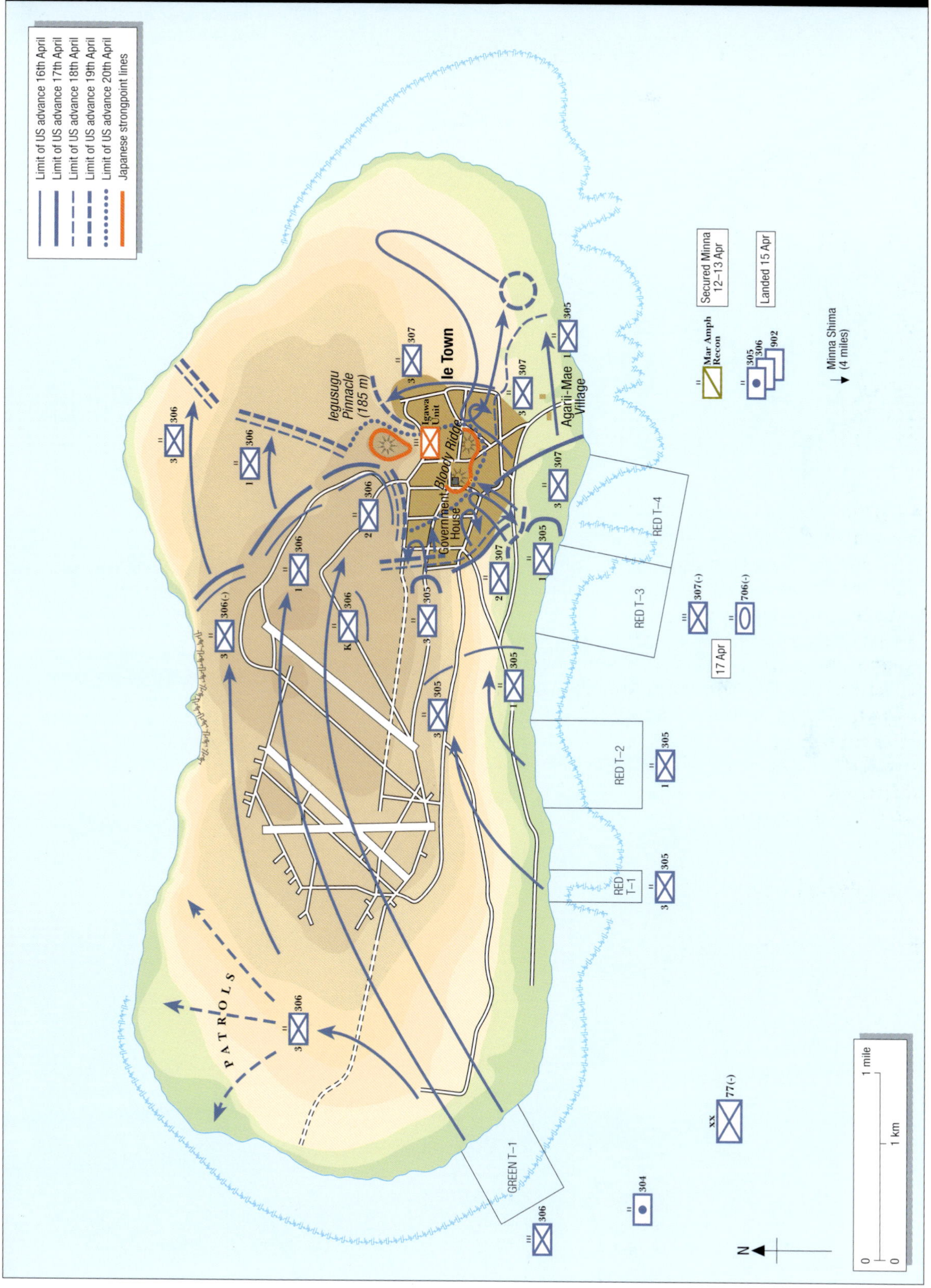

A Marine resupply point on southern Okinawa. Troops drew ammunition, demolitions, flamethrower fuel, water, and rations at such points as this rotated from reserve positions to the front. A 105-mm M7 self-propelled howitzer passes on its way to the front. An M4A3 Sherman tank can be seen to the rear. (USMC)

well-developed, but unsurfaced road network. Cultivated vegetable and sugarcane fields covered much of this land interspersed with clear areas of low grasses and clumps of scrub trees. Thrusting abruptly upward from the east portion of the island is Iegusugu Pinnacle. This is a conical limestone peak 600 ft (185 m) high, nicknamed "the Pinnacle" and covered with scrub brush and trees, and honeycombed with caves and ravines reinforced by tunnels and pillboxes. On the Pinnacle's south side is the sprawling Ie Town of stone buildings. On the island's center were three 6,000–7,000 ft (1,820–2,120 m) long airfields in the pattern of an "XI." The island had a population of 8,000, but about 3,000 had

Marines clear bodies, discarded weapons, and equipment from Sugar Loaf Hill, 23 May. A knocked-out M4A3 Sherman tank rests in the foreground. Two 105-mm M7 self-propelled howitzers pass two parked LVT(4)s that are transporting the dead. (USMC)

been evacuated to Okinawa. Ie Shima was defended by 3,000 troops of the Igawa Unit, augmented by 1,500 armed civilians including women. Substantial defenses were built around the Pinnacle and within Ie Town.

Minna Shima, an islet four miles (6.4 km) south of Ie, was secured by Fleet Marine Force, Pacific Reconnaissance Battalion troops on 12/13 April and occupied by the three artillery battalions (305, 306, 902 FA) on the 15th. The 77th Inf. Div. was moved from its station 300 miles (483 km) southeast of Okinawa and assaulted Ie Shima on the morning of 16 April (W-Day) with full naval gunfire support as well as artillery firing from Motobu Peninsula. The 306th Infantry landed on Beach "Green T-1" at 0758hrs (S-Hour) on the southwest end while the 305th Infantry (less 2nd Battalion) hit "Red T-1" and "T-2" on the south-central coast. Initially, as on Okinawa, there was virtually no resistance with the airfields soon overrun as the regiments swept east across the island toward the Pinnacle and Ie Town. Resistance increased the next day as the town was approached. The 307th Infantry (less 1st Battalion) was landed on the morning of 17 April with part of the 706th Tank Battalion on "Red T-3". By 18 April the troops had closed in on the north, west, and south sides of the town and Pinnacle amid accusations of taking too long to accomplish the mission. The repeated attacks bogged down against fierce resistance, especially in the town's center around the administrative building, called Government House Hill, and the surrounding high ground known as Bloody Ridge. Most of the town was cleared on 20 April but the Pinnacle was not taken until the next day, and resistance continued on its slopes until 23 April. Ie Shima was declared secure at 1730hrs on 21 April, but mopping-up continued until the 26th. The Japanese lost 4,700, including most of the 1,500 armed civilians, and 409 prisoners were taken. About a third of the civilians remaining on the island died. American losses were 218 dead and missing and 900 wounded. Tragically, the popular war correspondent Ernie Pyle was killed by machine-gun fire on 18 April. On 25–28 April the 77th Inf. Div. was moved to Okinawa and was soon in combat again. The 1/305 Infantry remained on the island mopping-up until relieved by 2/106 Infantry on 6 May. The 2/305 occupied Zamami Shima. The entire civilian population was removed from Ie Shima within two weeks of it being secured to prevent interference with airfield construction. They were returned after the war.

THE ASSAULT ON THE SHURI DEFENSES

On Okinawa Shima XXIV Corps' Army divisions were now facing the Japanese main cross-island defense line – the Shuri defenses – built on a series of steep ridges and escarpments to the north of Shuri. The 7th Inf. Div. was to the east, the 96th in the center, and the 27th to the west. They had not moved since 14 April as preparations for the 19 April assault were undertaken. The entire Japanese front was still defended by the 62nd Division with its 64th Brigade defending the west and center and the 63rd Brigade the east, well dug in on the hills and ridges, mainly the Urasoe-Mura Escarpment in the west and center and the Tanabaru Escarpment in the east. The 44th IMB was to the rear in the Shuri area.

A preliminary attack was launched by the 27th Inf. Div. on the night of 18 April when bridges were secretly built across the Machinato Inlet

separating Uchitomari and Machinato on the west coast. The 106th Infantry secured a valuable foothold on the northwest end of the Urasoe-Mura Escarpment and cleared Machinato Village during a bold night infiltration attack.

The main attack was launched at 0640hrs, 19 April, after a massive 27-battalion artillery barrage while naval gunfire and aircraft pounded the Japanese rear area. The 7th Inf. Div. attacked toward Skyline Ridge, the anchor at the east end of the Japanese line, but was thrown back in most sectors by withering fire. The 96th Inf. Div. in the center made little headway against the strongly defended Tombstone and Nishibaru Ridges, barely gaining any ground beyond its start line. The 27th Inf. Div. on the west flank

The bodies of two paratroopers of the Japanese 1st Raiding Brigade who attempted an airlanded raid on Yontan Airfield on the night of 24 May. The wreckage of aircraft they destroyed with demolitions and grenades litter the area. They managed to destroy eight fighters and damage 24. (US Army)

merely held its ground on the south side of the Machinato Inlet, but made further gains on the Urasoe-Mura Escarpment. Its attack on the Kakazu Ridge failed, however, when the 193rd Tank Battalion was separated from 1/105th Infantry as they crossed a saddle between Kakazu and Nishibaru Ridges, resulting in the loss of 22 tanks and the attack's failure.

For the next week the three divisions continued the effort to push south against well dug-in resistance with no unit gaining more than 1,300 yds (1,188 m). The 27th Inf. Div. on the west flank was stalled on the north side of Gusukuma near the coast and on its inland flank at the Urasoe-Mura Escarpment, as was the 96th Infantry Division. Kakazu and Nishibaru Ridges and the Tanabaru were overcome, but the Japanese 22nd Infantry was holding up the 7th Inf. Div. on the east flank. The Bradford Task Force, assembled from reserve battalions of all three divisions in the line, and heavily supported by armor, overran the Kakazu Pocket on 24 April, but the Japanese had abandoned it. The Japanese also lost their one opportunity for a successful counterattack as there were no US reserves; everything had been committed to the line. By the end of the month most units had progressed comparatively well, gaining 1,000–2,000 yds (914–1,829 m) in many areas. The 96th Inf. Div. was still held up on its west flank by the Urasoe-Mura Escarpment defended by the Japanese 32nd Infantry. The US 7th Inf. Div. had made significant headway on its inland flank, but was held up there on Kochi Ridge by the Japanese 22nd Infantry. The divisions were exhausted and their strength low.

It was during this period that it was proposed to execute a flanking landing using the 77th Inf. Div. on the southwest coast north of Minatogawa in an effort to force the Japanese to pull troops out of the Shuri defenses. It was rejected by Buckner from 17–22 April as it was too much of a risk to land a single division so far behind Japanese lines, with the additional logistics burden and the ships required to protect the supporting anchorage.

The 1st Mar. Div. was attached to XXIV Corps on 30 April, relieving the 27th Inf. Div. on the east flank. The 77th Inf. Div, although short

three battalions on occupation duty on outlying islands, relieved the much battered 96th. The assault continued southward through the main Shuri defenses, an effort continued until 3 May, when the Japanese attempted their most determined counteroffensive.

THE JAPANESE COUNTEROFFENSIVE

Frustrated at the prolonged defensive battle, many Japanese commanders desired a counteroffensive to halt the American advance. Colonel Yahara, 32nd Army operations officer, warned of the folly of such an attack, but Major-General Cho, chief-of-staff, prevailed. The Japanese attacked on the night of 3 May with their main effort made in the center and the east by the 24th Division. The attack was supported by raids conducted by forces landed in the American rear on both coasts. Shallow penetrations were accomplished in some areas, but the attack was repulsed (see the Bird's Eye View map on pp.74–75 for details of the counterattack). Japanese losses, some 7,000 of the 76,000-man force, only served to further weaken their front. American units had suffered fewer than 700 casualties and they continued to push south. The counteroffensive was nothing short of a blunder.

The Japanese now rebuilt their units, largely with rear service troops, and prepared for a battle of attrition. The 62nd Division, with only a quarter of its strength surviving, defended the western third of the line while the 24th Division, reduced to two-thirds, defended from north of Shuri to the east coast. The 44th IMB, at four-fifths strength, supported the 62nd Division. Japanese artillery had been cut by half and its daily ammunition allotment drastically reduced.

---

19 The Americans used Japanese place names when so identified on the map, but many terrain features were unnamed and given nicknames or named after a nearby village.

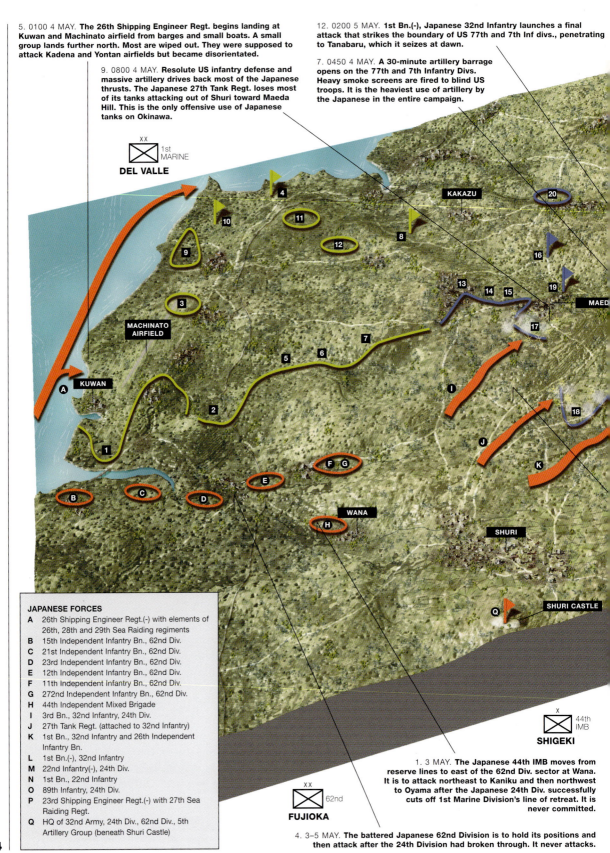

5. 0100 4 MAY. **The 26th Shipping Engineer Regt. begins landing at Kuwan and Machinato airfield from barges and small boats. A small group lands further north. Most are wiped out. They were supposed to attack Kadena and Yontan airfields but became disorientated.**

9. 0800 4 MAY. **Resolute US infantry defense and massive artillery drives back most of the Japanese thrusts. The Japanese 27th Tank Regt. loses most of its tanks attacking out of Shuri toward Maeda Hill. This is the only offensive use of Japanese tanks on Okinawa.**

12. 0200 5 MAY. **1st Bn.(-), Japanese 32nd Infantry launches a final attack that strikes the boundary of US 77th and 7th Inf divs., penetrating to Tanabaru, which it seizes at dawn.**

7. 0450 4 MAY. **A 30-minute artillery barrage opens on the 77th and 7th Infantry Divs. Heavy smoke screens are fired to blind US troops. It is the heaviest use of artillery by the Japanese in the entire campaign.**

XX
1st MARINE
DEL VALLE

KAKAZU

20

4

10

11

8

12

16

9

13

14 15

19

3

MAED

MACHINATO
AIRFIELD

7

5

6

17

A KUWAN

2

I

1

18

F G

E

J

B

C

D

K

WANA

H

SHURI

Q

SHURI CASTLE

JAPANESE FORCES

A 26th Shipping Engineer Regt.(-) with elements of 26th, 28th and 29th Sea Raiding regiments
B 15th Independent Infantry Bn., 62nd Div.
C 21st Independent Infantry Bn., 62nd Div.
D 23rd Independent Infantry Bn., 62nd Div.
E 12th Independent Infantry Bn., 62nd Div.
F 11th Independent Infantry Bn., 62nd Div.
G 272nd Independent Infantry Bn., 62nd Div.
H 44th Independent Mixed Brigade
I 3rd Bn., 32nd Infantry, 24th Div.
J 27th Tank Regt. (attached to 32nd Infantry)
K 1st Bn., 32nd Infantry and 26th Independent Infantry Bn.
L 1st Bn.(-), 32nd Infantry
M 22nd Infantry(-), 24th Div.
N 1st Bn., 22nd Infantry
O 89th Infantry, 24th Div.
P 23rd Shipping Engineer Regt.(-) with 27th Sea Raiding Regt.
Q HQ of 32nd Army, 24th Div., 62nd Div., 5th Artillery Group (beneath Shuri Castle)

X
44th IMB
SHIGEKI

1. 3 MAY. **The Japanese 44th IMB moves from reserve lines to east of the 62nd Div. sector at Wana. It is to attack northeast to Kaniku and then northwest to Oyama after the Japanese 24th Div. successfully cuts off 1st Marine Division's line of retreat. It is never committed.**

XX
62nd
FUJIOKA

4. 3–5 MAY. **The battered Japanese 62nd Division is to hold its positions and then attack after the 24th Division had broken through. It never attacks.**

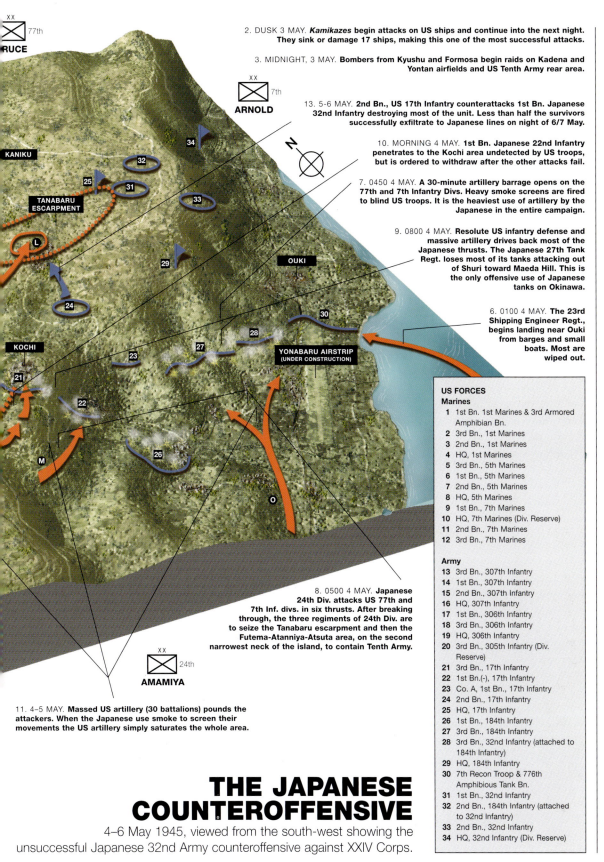

2. DUSK 3 MAY. *Kamikazes* begin attacks on US ships and continue into the next night. They sink or damage 17 ships, making this one of the most successful attacks.

3. MIDNIGHT, 3 MAY. Bombers from Kyushu and Formosa begin raids on Kadena and Yontan airfields and US Tenth Army rear area.

XX
7th
ARNOLD

13. 5-6 MAY. 2nd Bn., US 17th Infantry counterattacks 1st Bn. Japanese 32nd Infantry destroying most of the unit. Less than half the survivors successfully exfiltrate to Japanese lines on night of 6/7 May.

10. MORNING 4 MAY. 1st Bn. Japanese 22nd Infantry penetrates to the Kochi area undetected by US troops, but is ordered to withdraw after the other attacks fail.

34

KANIKU

7. 0450 4 MAY. A 30-minute artillery barrage opens on the 77th and 7th Infantry Divs. Heavy smoke screens are fired to blind US troops. It is the heaviest use of artillery by the Japanese in the entire campaign.

32

25   31

TANABARU
ESCARPMENT

33

L

9. 0800 4 MAY. Resolute US infantry defense and massive artillery drives back most of the Japanese thrusts. The Japanese 27th Tank Regt. loses most of its tanks attacking out of Shuri toward Maeda Hill. This is the only offensive use of Japanese tanks on Okinawa.

29   OUKI

24

30

6. 0100 4 MAY. The 23rd Shipping Engineer Regt., begins landing near Ouki from barges and small boats. Most are wiped out.

28

KOCHI

23   27

21

22   YONABARU AIRSTRIP
(UNDER CONSTRUCTION)

M   26

O

8. 0500 4 MAY. Japanese 24th Div. attacks US 77th and 7th Inf. divs. in six thrusts. After breaking through, the three regiments of 24th Div. are to seize the Tanabaru escarpment and then the Futema-Atanniya-Atsuta area, on the second narrowest neck of the island, to contain Tenth Army.

XX
24th
AMAMIYA

11. 4–5 MAY. Massed US artillery (30 battalions) pounds the attackers. When the Japanese use smoke to screen their movements the US artillery simply saturates the whole area.

US FORCES
Marines
1   1st Bn. 1st Marines & 3rd Armored Amphibian Bn.
2   3rd Bn., 1st Marines
3   2nd Bn., 1st Marines
4   HQ, 1st Marines
5   3rd Bn., 5th Marines
6   1st Bn., 5th Marines
7   2nd Bn., 5th Marines
8   HQ, 5th Marines
9   1st Bn., 7th Marines
10   HQ, 7th Marines (Div. Reserve)
11   2nd Bn., 7th Marines
12   3rd Bn., 7th Marines
Army
13   3rd Bn., 307th Infantry
14   1st Bn., 307th Infantry
15   2nd Bn., 307th Infantry
16   HQ, 307th Infantry
17   1st Bn., 306th Infantry
18   3rd Bn., 306th Infantry
19   HQ, 306th Infantry
20   3rd Bn., 305th Infantry (Div. Reserve)
21   3rd Bn., 17th Infantry
22   1st Bn.(-), 17th Infantry
23   Co. A, 1st Bn., 17th Infantry
24   2nd Bn., 17th Infantry
25   HQ, 17th Infantry
26   1st Bn., 184th Infantry
27   3rd Bn., 184th Infantry
28   3rd Bn., 32nd Infantry (attached to 184th Infantry)
29   HQ, 184th Infantry
30   7th Recon Troop & 776th Amphibious Tank Bn.
31   1st Bn., 32nd Infantry
32   2nd Bn., 184th Infantry (attached to 32nd Infantry)
33   2nd Bn., 32nd Infantry
34   HQ, 32nd Infantry (Div. Reserve)

THE JAPANESE COUNTEROFFENSIVE

4–6 May 1945, viewed from the south-west showing the unsuccessful Japanese 32nd Army counteroffensive against XXIV Corps.

ACTION AT SEA

Throughout the campaign TF 51 (Joint Expeditionary Force) provided close air support to the troops ashore, combat air patrols to protect from air attacks, interception of *Kamikazes*, reconnaissance and anti-submarine patrols, logistical support, floating hospitals, continuous gun fire support, and other indispensable services.

The first two weeks of the campaign saw TF 57 (British Carrier Force) operating off Saishima Gunto to neutralize airfields there. Prior to and during the campaign, the Fifth and Third Fleets' fast carriers executed attacks throughout the Ryukyus, on Formosa, mainland China, and Kyushu to neutralize Japanese airfields.

KAMIKAZE ATTACKS

The *Kamikaze,* or Special Attack, concept of intentional suicide attacks on Allied ships by volunteer pilots originated in the Philippines. Those early attacks were sporadically planned, but by the time of Okinawa a well-organized effort had been developed; *Ten-Go* Operation. The 1st Special Attack Force, under Admiral Soemu Toyoda, consisted of over 1,800 aircraft of the combined 5th Air Fleet and 6th Air Army based on Kyushu and Formosa. The Force launched its first attacks in mid-March during the fast carrier raids on Japan. Limited attacks were launched during the initial Okinawa landings, but the full fury of the *Kamikaze* was not felt until a massive 355-plane raid on 6–7 April was unleashed. In 19 hours the Navy suffered six ships sunk and 21 damaged with over 500 casualties. The Japanese lost almost 400 aircraft; *Kamikaze* and conventional covering fighters. The attacks continued unabated through April with a total of 14 US ships sunk and 90 damaged by *Kamikazes*, while conventional air attacks sank one and damaged 47. The Japanese paid a price of over 1,100 aircraft. The month of May saw more air attacks, which concentrated on the picket ships, transports, and carriers as well as the American airfields. Especially heavy attacks occurred in late May. Attacks continued to the end of the campaign, with the last launched on 21–22 June. In all there were ten main attacks, *Sho-Go 1* to *10,* with 1,465 aircraft interspersed with smaller attacks to total about 1,900 aircraft. The result was 26 US ships sunk and 225 damaged by *Kamikazes* as well as two sunk and 61 damaged by conventional air attack. The attacks on the fleet caused the highest US Navy casualty rate in the war.

Among the *Kamikazes* was the MXY7 *Ohka* (Cherry Blossom) rocket-propelled, manned bomb, better known by its American nickname, the *Baka* (Fool) bomb. Dropped from IJN G4M "Betty" twin-engine bombers, the first attack taking place on 21 March, only one ship was sunk and four damaged by the 2,646-lb (1,200-kg) guided bomb.

Dark blue-painted F4U-1 Corsair fighters of Marine Fighting Squadron 232 (VMF-232) roll in over southern Okinawa to hit ground targets. Close air support of ground troops was one of the main missions of Marine aviation. (US Army)

THE SINKING OF THE *YAMATO*

In a desperate effort the Japanese sortied the *Yamato* on 6 April on a suicide mission. The super battleship was to beach itself on Okinawa to the south of the American landing beaches and turn its 18.1-in. guns on American forces ashore and the transports. There was only enough fuel available for the *Yamato* and its accompanying ships to make a one-way trip. The *Ten-Ichi* Operation ("Heaven Number One") saw the *Yamato*, the light cruiser *Yahagi,* and eight destroyers sortie from Tokuyama Naval Base on southwest Honshu. One destroyer experienced engine trouble and turned back. Vice-Admiral Seiichi Ito's Surface Special Attack Force was detected by US submarines soon after it entered the open sea. Contact was lost during the night as the force turned west. American carrier planes found the *Yamato* on the morning of 7 April after it had turned southwest toward its target. TF 58 aircraft struck the force at noon, sinking the *Yamato* (ten torpedo, five bomb hits), the *Yahagi,* (seven torpedo, 12 bomb hits), and four destroyers in two hours at a cost of ten US aircraft. Without air cover the battleship did not even make it halfway to Okinawa and went down with 2,487 crew. Four damaged escort destroyers escaped back to Japan.

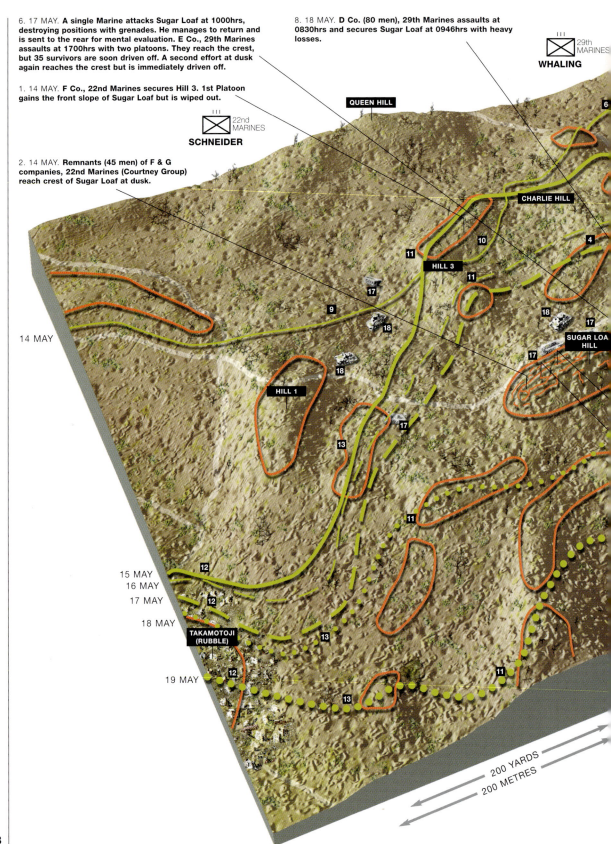

6. 17 MAY. **A single Marine attacks Sugar Loaf at 1000hrs, destroying positions with grenades. He manages to return and is sent to the rear for mental evaluation. E Co., 29th Marines assaults at 1700hrs with two platoons. They reach the crest, but 35 survivors are soon driven off. A second effort at dusk again reaches the crest but is immediately driven off.**

8. 18 MAY. **D Co. (80 men), 29th Marines assaults at 0830hrs and secures Sugar Loaf at 0946hrs with heavy losses.**

1. 14 MAY. **F Co., 22nd Marines secures Hill 3. 1st Platoon gains the front slope of Sugar Loaf but is wiped out.**

2. 14 MAY. **Remnants (45 men) of F & G companies, 22nd Marines (Courtney Group) reach crest of Sugar Loaf at dusk.**

29th MARINES
WHALING

QUEEN HILL

22nd MARINES
SCHNEIDER

CHARLIE HILL

10

4

11

HILL 3

11

17

9

18

18

17

SUGAR LOA HILL

17

14 MAY

HILL 1

17

13

11

12

15 MAY
16 MAY
17 MAY

12

18 MAY

TAKAMOTOJI (RUBBLE)

13

11

19 MAY

12

13

200 YARDS
200 METRES

78

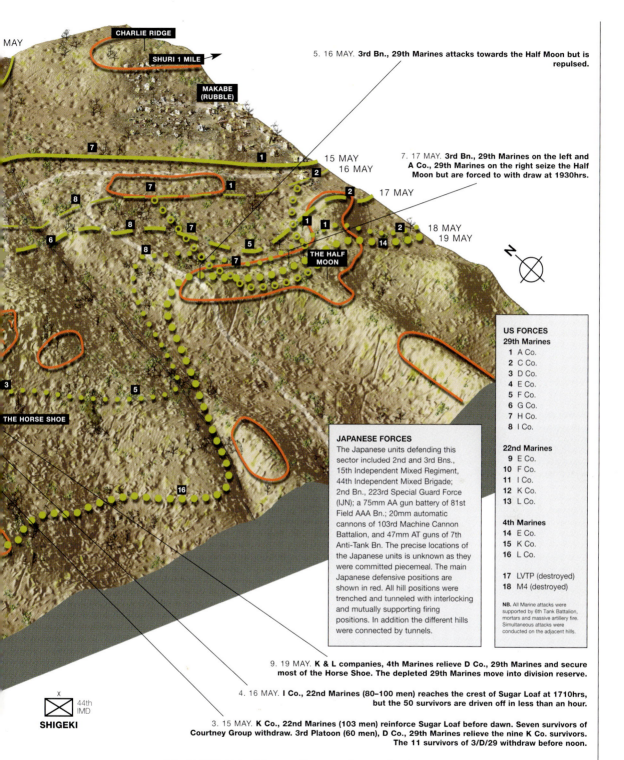

MAY

CHARLIE RIDGE

SHURI 1 MILE →

MAKABE
(RUBBLE)

5. 16 MAY. 3rd Bn., 29th Marines attacks towards the Half Moon but is repulsed.

15 MAY
16 MAY

7. 17 MAY. 3rd Bn., 29th Marines on the left and A Co., 29th Marines on the right seize the Half Moon but are forced to with draw at 1930hrs.

17 MAY

18 MAY
19 MAY

THE HALF
MOON

THE HORSE SHOE

N

US FORCES
29th Marines
1 A Co.
2 C Co.
3 D Co.
4 E Co.
5 F Co.
6 G Co.
7 H Co.
8 I Co.

22nd Marines
9 E Co.
10 F Co.
11 I Co.
12 K Co.
13 L Co.

4th Marines
14 E Co.
15 K Co.
16 L Co.

17 LVTP (destroyed)
18 M4 (destroyed)

NB. All Marine attacks were supported by 6th Tank Battalion, mortars and massive artillery fire. Simultaneous attacks were conducted on the adjacent hills.

JAPANESE FORCES
The Japanese units defending this sector included 2nd and 3rd Bns., 15th Independent Mixed Regiment, 44th Independent Mixed Brigade; 2nd Bn., 223rd Special Guard Force (IJN); a 75mm AA gun battery of 81st Field AAA Bn.; 20mm automatic cannons of 103rd Machine Cannon Battalion, and 47mm AT guns of 7th Anti-Tank Bn. The precise locations of the Japanese units is unknown as they were committed piecemeal. The main Japanese defensive positions are shown in red. All hill positions were trenched and tunneled with interlocking and mutually supporting firing positions. In addition the different hills were connected by tunnels.

X
44th
IMD

SHIGEKI

9. 19 MAY. K & L companies, 4th Marines relieve D Co., 29th Marines and secure most of the Horse Shoe. The depleted 29th Marines move into division reserve.

4. 16 MAY. I Co., 22nd Marines (80–100 men) reaches the crest of Sugar Loaf at 1710hrs, but the 50 survivors are driven off in less than an hour.

3. 15 MAY. K Co., 22nd Marines (103 men) reinforce Sugar Loaf before dawn. Seven survivors of Courtney Group withdraw. 3rd Platoon (60 men), D Co., 29th Marines relieve the nine K Co. survivors. The 11 survivors of 3/D/29 withdraw before noon.

BATTLE FOR SUGAR LOAF HILL

13–19 May 1945, viewed from the south-west showing the initial 6th Marine Division assaults on Sugar Loaf Hill, the key to breaching the west flank of the Shuri Line. It required seven days to advance 520 yards. More than 3,000 Marines and untold thousands of Japanese were killed or wounded.

SEIZING THE SOUTH

SHURI FALLS

On 7 May, IIIAC resumed control of the 1st Marine Division on the west flank. As the Americans pushed south the island widened and it would be necessary to place a fourth division into the line. The 6th Mar. Div. was soon assigned a sector on the 1st Mar. Div.'s right and inserted a single regiment, the 22nd, into the line. The 77th Inf. Div. was strengthened by the arrival of its understrength 305th Infantry, relieved from garrisoning Ie Shima. The rested 96th Inf. Div. relieved the 7th Inf. Div. in the line on 8 May (the surrender of Germany was announced that day). The Tenth Army's renewed offensive began on 11 May with, from east to west, 96th Inf., 77th Inf., 1st Mar., and 6th Mar. divisions in the line.

There had been rain earlier but on 22 May heavy rains began. After ten days low ground, gullies, and ravines turned into thigh-deep seas of mud. Small streams and rivers overflowed their banks and the already overburdened roads became impassable in many areas.

The primary objective was Shuri. Progress was slow but steady, although the two center divisions had not driven as deeply into the Shuri defenses as those on the flanks. The 6th Mar. Div. was held up by furious fighting around Sugar Loaf Hill west of Shuri as the other divisions battled for stoutly defended ridges and hills. No complete Japanese unit remained in the lines, only remnants. On 29 May the 22nd Marines took Naha while an element of the 5th Marines, seizing the opportunity, crossed into the 77th Infantry Division's sector and captured Shuri Castle, much to the Army's exasperation. On the same date Army units broke through on the east coast as Japanese units were

A 4th Marines, 6th Mar. Div. .30cal. M1919A4 machine-gun squad maintains covering fire for assault troops on the southern portion of Oroku Peninsula as they enter the central hills, 7 June. (USMC)

ABOVE **A 4.2-in. M2 mortar of the Army's 91st Chemical Mortar Company (Separate) fires in support of the 22nd Marines, 6th Mar. Div., 18 June. The Marines, lacking such mortars, valued their support as they could quickly place high explosives and white phosphorus smoke on targets. (USMC)**

ABOVE, RIGHT **Seeing their still experimental first use in the Pacific, these Army 75-mm T25 recoilless rifles are being bore-sighted before going into action. They were mounted on the same tripod as the .30cal. M1917A1 heavy machine gun. The weapons could be man-packed relatively easily into terrain not accessible to heavier weapons. They were extremely accurate, making them valuable for knocking out caves and pillboxes. A small number of shoulder-fired 57-mm T15E1 recoilless rifles were also used. (US Army)**

routed creating a melee of intermingled US and Japanese units, with many units at times being attacked from both sides. The apparent confusion was due to a complex Japanese scheme of withdrawal.

THE PUSH SOUTH

On 25 May, the Japanese 62nd Division withdrew through a defensive line of the 44th IMB southeast of Naha and then attacked XXIV Corps elements to the east. The Japanese 24th Division then withdrew from that sector on 29 May as the 62nd Division established a new line to the rear. The 24th Division established a new line south of Itoman on the west coast as the 44th IMB withdrew on 31 May to establish a line linked to the 24th Division's and running to the east coast. The 62nd Division then conducted a fighting withdrawal through the new lines between 30 May and 4 June. The 10,000-man Naval Base Force on Oroku Peninsula, misinterpreting the order, withdrew to the south too early on 28 May. Dissatisfied with the positions there, they immediately returned to their base, preferring to die defending it rather than flight alongside the Imperial Japanese Army. US aerial observers, sighting large numbers of the enemy moving south and service troops moving north to reinforce the withdrawing units, thought that the Japanese were merely using the poor weather to mask a relief of line units. The Japanese 32nd Army successfully withdrew to the south, but of the 50,000 troops at the beginning of the operation, only 30,000 remained. Those wounded capable of action had been left behind to fight to the death with the rearguards, and the severely wounded were killed. The 32nd Army Headquarters left its tunnel command post beneath Shuri Castle on 27 May. It established a temporary CP at Tsukazan the next day and the following day moved to a small ridge (Hill 89) near Mabuni on the south coast. Heavy spring rains began at this time, arriving two weeks later than normal. Rains hindered both sides' operations, but the vehicle-dependent Americans were hampered most.

On 24 May paratroopers of the Japanese 1st Raiding Brigade attempted an airlanded raid on Yontan Airfield staged from Japan. Only

one of the five transports managed to land. A number of US aircraft were destroyed and damaged on the ground, but the raiders were quickly killed.

IJN forces still held the Oroku Peninsula on the southwest coast, south of Naha (*Brother*), where the 6th Mar. Div. was blocked by Naha Harbor. Not to be halted by a mere body of water, the Division did what was natural and executed a shore-to-shore amphibious assault launched from the west coast north of Naha and into Naha Harbor to flank enemy forces on the peninsula on 4 June (K-Day).

The 4th Marines landed on Beaches "Red 1" and "Red 2", south of Naha, at 0600hrs to be followed by the 29th Marines. While not given much attention, the two-regiment subsidiary operation was larger than some earlier amphibious assaults. It was also the last opposed amphibious assault in World War Two.

The 2nd Mar. Div.'s 8th Marines returned to Okinawa from Saipan on 30 May. Its 2nd and 3rd Battalions landed on Iheya Jima on 3 June and the 1st Battalion landed on Aguni Shima on 9 June. These islands,

A gunner of the 22nd Marines, 6th Mar. Div. turns a 7.7-mm Model 92 (1932) machine gun against its former owners. This was a copy of the British World War One-vintage Lewis machine gun used by the Imperial Japanese Navy. Its 47-round drum magazines and extra cartons of ammunition lie on the ground. (USMC)

north and west of Okinawa, were unoccupied. Radar and fighter direction centers were established on both islands.

The situation was stabilized by 31 May with most Japanese rear guards positioned in the central portion of the crumbling lines. By 3 June the 7th Inf. Div. had pushed south on to the Chinen Peninsula on the southeast coast. The 96th Inf. Div. and 1st Mar. Div. steadily drove south in the center as the 6th Marine Division cleared the Oroku Peninsula on the west coast.

THE LAST STAND

After hard fighting, the Japanese remnants were driven to the south end of the island, Kiyan Peninsula, by 11 June. There were still substantial pockets in the American rear areas. The Japanese intent now was to hold a line running from south of Itoman on the west coast through the Yuza-Dake and Yaeju-Dake hill masses in the center to a point on the east coast south of Minatogawa, an area approximately five miles across and three deep. The 8th Marines landed at Naha on 15 June and was attached to the 1st Mar. Div. to assist with the final operations ashore. The Tenth Army commander, Lieutenant-General Buckner, was killed observing his troops' advance against the final organized resistance on 18 June. Major-General Roy Geiger assumed command of Tenth Army, the only Marine officer to command a field army, while retaining command of IIIAC. The next day he was promoted to lieutenant-general. General Buckner had expressly picked Geiger to assume command in the event of his death. Five days later Geiger was relieved by Army Lieutenant-General Joseph W. Stilwell.

The assaulting divisions' sectors had narrowed to the point that only three to five of the freshest battalions were required in the line. The 7th Inf. Div. overran the Japanese 44th IMB's pocket on Hill 115 southwest of Nakaza on 17 June. The US 96th Inf. Div. was pinched out of the line on 20 June to deal with a large pocket of Japanese 24th Division in the peninsula's center at Medeera and Makabe. It was not reduced until 22 June. As the 6th Mar. Div. cleared the west coast of the peninsula, the 1st Mar. Div. wiped out the remaining Japanese 62nd Division pocket just inland of the island's south end on the Kiyamu-Gusuku Ridge. The 7th Inf. Div. closed in on the Japanese 32nd Army's Headquarters, defended by 24th Division survivors, on a coastal ridge (Hill 89) south of Mabuni. These pockets were largely wiped out on 21 June and Okinawa Shoito was declared secure at 1700hrs. Small pockets of resistance remained and the American mopping-up continued for days. At 0340hrs 22 June, Lieutenant-General Ushijima and Major-General Cho committed ritual suicide outside their cave on the south side of Hill 89. The other division and brigade commanders and staffs died during "honorable death attacks" between 21 and 30 June.

Kume Shima, 55 miles (89 km) west of Okinawa, was secured by the Fleet Marine Force, Pacific Amphibious Reconnaissance Battalion between 26 and 30 June to establish a radar site and fighter direction center. Landing on the island's southeast coast, the force met no opposition from the estimated 50-man garrison, which was later engaged. This was the final amphibious assault of World War Two.

AFTERMATH

The armed forces of America and Japan had met in an 82-day, no quarter battle, proving what was already known by both sides: the victor would have to utterly destroy his opponent. Both sides used their resources, whether limited or abundant, to the utmost of their ability to achieve their goals and gain the tactical advantage. Okinawa provided a glimpse of what would have happened if the United States had been forced to invade the Japanese Home Islands.

Only the much larger and longer Philippine Campaign saw higher casualties in the Pacific Theater than Okinawa. Marine ground and air losses were 2,938 dead and missing and 16,017 wounded. The Army lost 4,675 dead and missing and 18,099 wounded. There were over 26,200 US casualties due to combat fatigue, illness, and non-battle injuries. The joint US air services lost 763 aircraft, 458 in combat. US Navy losses were inordinately high with 36 ships sunk and 368 damaged, of which 43 were so badly damaged they were scrapped. These high rates were largely due to the suicide attacks on the fleet. These attacks were also the cause of the Navy's highest casualty rate of the war – 4,900 dead and missing and 4,800 wounded. The British Carrier Force (TF 57) suffered four ships damaged, 98 aircraft lost, 62 KIA, and 82 WIA.

The seven US divisions and IIIAC and XXIV Corps troops suffered the losses listed in the table below. To replace these losses Army units received 12,227 replacements and the Marines 11,147. Tenth Army troops and TAF are not included.

ARMY AND MARINE CORPS CASUALTIES

Division	KIA/DOW	WIA/IIA	MIA	Total
1st Mar. Div.	1,067	6,418	40	6,525
2nd Mar. Div.*	8/48	37/327	8/1	423
6th Mar. Div.	1,622	6,689	15	7,326
7th Inf. Div.	1,122	4,943	3	6,068
27th Inf. Div.	711	2,520	24	3,255
77th Inf. Div.	1,018	3,968	40	5,026
96th Inf. Div.	1,506	5,912	12	7,430
IIIAC	35	149	4	188
XXIV Corps	55	346	2	403

* Two sets of casualty figures are provided for the 2nd Mar. Div. The first number represents 3/2 Marines' losses during the L-Day demonstration and the second is the 8th Marines' losses while attached to the 1st Mar. Div. in June.

Over 100,000 Japanese troops and Okinawan *Boeitai* fought on Okinawa and other islands in the Ryukyus. Estimates of casualties are difficult to determine due to the duration of the action, numbers of enemy forces, inflated reporting of enemy dead, and the nature of combat on Okinawa. The US assessment of Japanese casualties came to over 142,000, more than were on the island. A more realistic assessment is that approximately

An exhausted marine rests on shell-blasted ground during the final stages of the last battle of World War II. (USMC)

66,000 combatants died and half of the survivors were wounded. A total of 7,400 combatants were taken prisoner during the campaign. Some 3,400 unarmed laborers (*Boeitai*, Koreans, and Chinese) were captured. Large numbers of troops turned themselves in after Japan surrendered. Approximately 10,000 IJA and IJN personnel and 8,000 Okinawan *Boeitai* and conscripts survived the battle. The Japanese lost 7,830 aircraft; 4,155 in combat, 2,655 operationally, and 1,020 destroyed on the ground on Kyushu and Formosa. Over 4,600 *Kamikaze* crews died along with hundreds of other pilots. Over 3,650 IJN sailors were lost during the *Yamato*'s sortie. Japan lost a total of 16 warships during the campaign with four damaged.

Island Command's military government and military police took charge of 285,272 Okinawan and Japanese civilians. At the conclusion of the operation, 42,000–50,000 Okinawan civilians were estimated to have died due to Japanese or American combat action or suicide, or were murdered by the Japanese (to prevent their surrender or to steal their food). Post-war studies found that over 122,000 civilians were killed (almost one-third of the indigenous population and a figure rivaling the combined death toll of over 120,000 at Hiroshima and Nagasaki) and a culture was shattered.

Ie Shima served a final role in the war when two white-painted Japanese G4M1 "Betty" bombers bearing green crosses in place of the rising sun arrived from Tokyo on 19 August with the Japanese surrender delegation. They were then flown to Manila on US aircraft. They returned the next day and set off for Japan. Because of misunderstandings, the American ground crew failed to provide sufficient fuel for the aircraft to return, and one crashed offshore of Japan, but the envoys were rescued and delivered the terms of unconditional surrender to the Emperor on schedule.

Large numbers of Japanese troops were killed in post-operation mopping-up and additional prisoners were taken, ultimately growing to 16,350 by the end of November 1945. It was the first time that large numbers of Japanese troops willingly surrendered. On 16 August, Japan announced its intention to surrender. On 29 August, those IJN troops still holding out in the Kerama Retto were among the first Japanese troops to surrender after the announcement. On 7 September, five days after V-J Day, the Ryukyu Islands were formerly surrendered at Kadena Airfield to Lieutenant-General Stilwell by Vice-Admiral Tadao Kato and Lieutenant-General Toshiro Nomi (both had been stationed in Sakishima Gunto). There were still approximately 105,000 IJA and IJN personnel on the other Ryukyus islands. Small numbers of Japanese renegades and Okinawan rebels conducted a low-level guerrilla war against US occupation forces into 1947 when the last surrendered.

The United States now possessed a base just 320 miles (515 km) southwest of Kyushu. A massive construction project began with 87,000

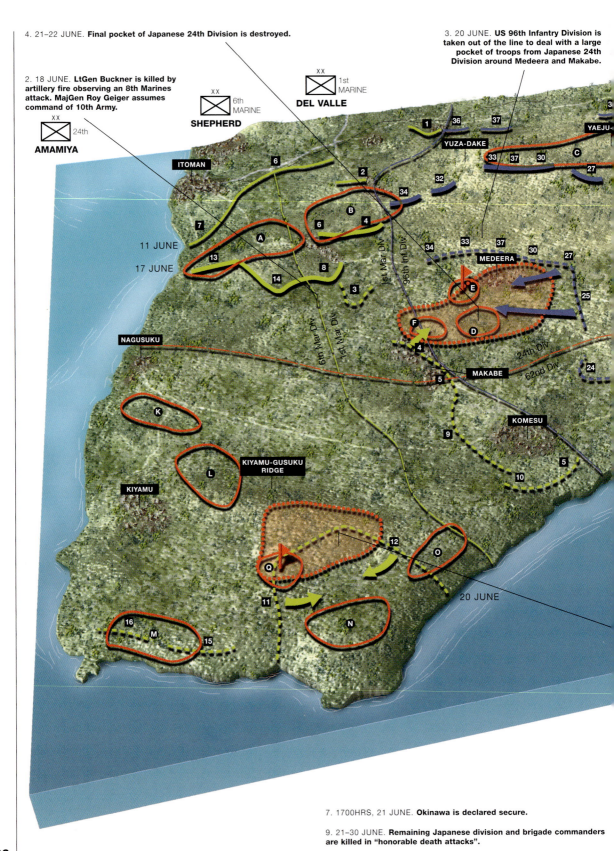

4. 21–22 JUNE. **Final pocket of Japanese 24th Division is destroyed.**

3. 20 JUNE. **US 96th Infantry Division is taken out of the line to deal with a large pocket of troops from Japanese 24th Division around Medeera and Makabe.**

2. 18 JUNE. **LtGen Buckner is killed by artillery fire observing an 8th Marines attack. MajGen Roy Geiger assumes command of 10th Army.**

XX
6th
MARINE
SHEPHERD

XX
1st
MARINE
DEL VALLE

XX
24th
AMAMIYA

ITOMAN

6

7

A

13

14

B

6

4

2

34

1

36

37

YUZA-DAKE

33   37   30

32

34

33

37

30

MEDEERA

27

YAEJU-

C

27

11 JUNE

17 JUNE

8

3

E

F

D

25

NAGUSUKU

1st Mar Div

96th Inf Div

6th Mar Div

1st Mar Div

4

5

MAKABE

24th Div

62nd Div

24

KOMESU

9

5

10

KIYAMU-GUSUKU RIDGE

K

L

KIYAMU

12

O

Q

11

N

16

M

15

20 JUNE

7. 1700HRS, 21 JUNE. **Okinawa is declared secure.**

9. 21–30 JUNE. **Remaining Japanese division and brigade commanders are killed in "honorable death attacks".**

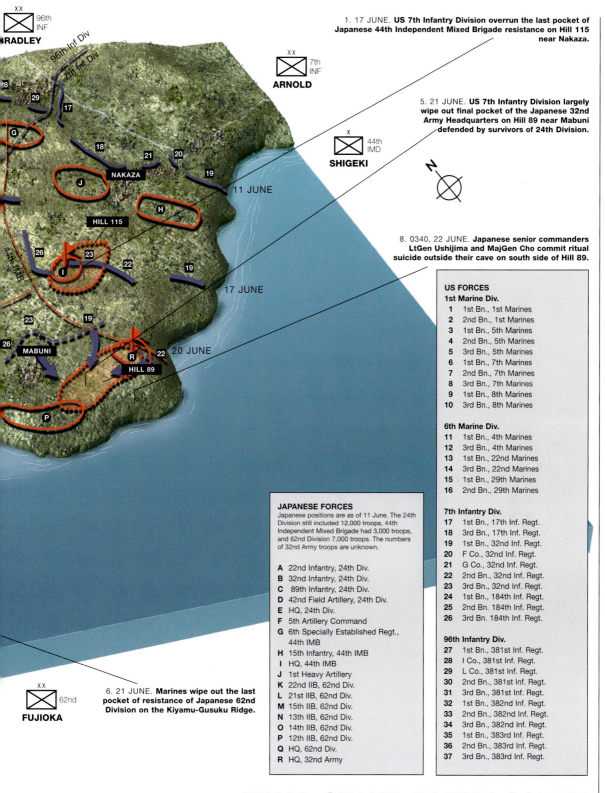

XX
96th
INF
BRADLEY

96th Inf Div
7th Inf Div

XX
7th
INF
ARNOLD

X
44th
IMD
SHIGEKI

XX
62nd
FUJIOKA

1. 17 JUNE. US 7th Infantry Division overrun the last pocket of Japanese 44th Independent Mixed Brigade resistance on Hill 115 near Nakaza.

5. 21 JUNE. US 7th Infantry Division largely wipe out final pocket of the Japanese 32nd Army Headquarters on Hill 89 near Mabuni defended by survivors of 24th Division.

8. 0340, 22 JUNE. Japanese senior commanders LtGen Ushijima and MajGen Cho commit ritual suicide outside their cave on south side of Hill 89.

6. 21 JUNE. Marines wipe out the last pocket of resistance of Japanese 62nd Division on the Kiyamu-Gusuku Ridge.

N

NAKAZA
HILL 115
MABUNI
HILL 89

11 JUNE
17 JUNE
20 JUNE

JAPANESE FORCES
Japanese positions are as of 11 June. The 24th Division still included 12,000 troops, 44th Independent Mixed Brigade had 3,000 troops, and 62nd Division 7,000 troops. The numbers of 32nd Army troops are unknown.

A 22nd Infantry, 24th Div.
B 32nd Infantry, 24th Div.
C 89th Infantry, 24th Div.
D 42nd Field Artillery, 24th Div.
E HQ, 24th Div.
F 5th Artillery Command
G 6th Specially Established Regt., 44th IMB
H 15th Infantry, 44th IMB
I HQ, 44th IMB
J 1st Heavy Artillery
K 22nd IIB, 62nd Div.
L 21st IIB, 62nd Div.
M 15th IIB, 62nd Div.
N 13th IIB, 62nd Div.
O 14th IIB, 62nd Div.
P 12th IIB, 62nd Div.
Q HQ, 62nd Div.
R HQ, 32nd Army

US FORCES
1st Marine Div.
1 1st Bn., 1st Marines
2 2nd Bn., 1st Marines
3 1st Bn., 5th Marines
4 2nd Bn., 5th Marines
5 3rd Bn., 5th Marines
6 1st Bn., 7th Marines
7 2nd Bn., 7th Marines
8 3rd Bn., 7th Marines
9 1st Bn., 8th Marines
10 3rd Bn., 8th Marines

6th Marine Div.
11 1st Bn., 4th Marines
12 3rd Bn., 4th Marines
13 1st Bn., 22nd Marines
14 3rd Bn., 22nd Marines
15 1st Bn., 29th Marines
16 2nd Bn., 29th Marines

7th Infantry Div.
17 1st Bn., 17th Inf. Regt.
18 3rd Bn., 17th Inf. Regt.
19 1st Bn., 32nd Inf. Regt.
20 F Co., 32nd Inf. Regt.
21 G Co., 32nd Inf. Regt.
22 2nd Bn., 32nd Inf. Regt.
23 3rd Bn., 32nd Inf. Regt.
24 1st Bn., 184th Inf. Regt.
25 2nd Bn. 184th Inf. Regt.
26 3rd Bn. 184th Inf. Regt.

96th Infantry Div.
27 1st Bn., 381st Inf. Regt.
28 I Co., 381st Inf. Regt.
29 L Co., 381st Inf. Regt.
30 2nd Bn. 381st Inf. Regt.
31 3rd Bn. 381st Inf. Regt.
32 1st Bn., 382nd Inf. Regt.
33 2nd Bn., 382nd Inf. Regt.
34 3rd Bn., 382nd Inf. Regt.
35 1st Bn., 383rd Inf. Regt.
36 2nd Bn., 383rd Inf. Regt.
37 3rd Bn., 383rd Inf. Regt.

FINAL STAND IN THE SOUTH
11–21 June 1945, viewed from the south-west showing the final Japanese defense of the Kiyan peninsula on Okinawa's southern end and the Tenth Army's assault on the Yaeju-Dake line.

construction troops (US Army, Navy, and Royal Engineers), who planned to build 22 airfields to accommodate the Eighth Air Force deploying from Europe as well as Navy and Marine aviation units. Only a proportion of the fields were completed, among them six 10,000-ft (3,048-m) bomber fields. Navy and Marine fields were established at Awase and Chimu on Okinawa and Plumb Field on Ie Shima. These fields were known collectively as Naval Air Stations, Okinawa.

Naval Operating Base, Okinawa, was established at Baten Ko on the south end of Buckner Bay, the renamed Nakagusuku Wan. It controlled port facilities at Naha, Chimu Wan, Nago Wan, and Katchin Hanto on the north end of Buckner Bay. The island developed into a major staging base for Army and Marine units destined for the invasion of Japan. Two devastating typhoons in September and October caused major damage and forced the relocation of some naval base facilities. The main naval base was moved from Baten Ko to the southeast end of the Katchin Peninsula to what is still known as "White" Beach. The 1950–53 Korean War made Okinawa an important Army logistics and Navy operating base as did Vietnam into the 1970s.

The Army Air Forces maintained a major bomber base at Kadena Air Base and the US Air Force continued to do so when organized in 1947. B-29 bombers flew long-range missions to bomb North Korea during the Korean War. B-52 bombers habitually flew missions to Vietnam from Okinawa and strategic reconnaissance aircraft operated from there on missions throughout Asia. In 1973 the Navy moved its facilities from Naha Air Base to Kadena Air Base to locate alongside the Air Force.

As combat units departed for the States after the war, the 44th Infantry, Philippine Scouts (a US Army unit composed of Filipino troops) garrisoned the island in January 1947, leading to racial disputes. The 44th Infantry left in May 1949 and was replaced by the US Army's 29th Infantry to guard the air bases. Army, Air Force, and Navy units have remained on the island since, and Marine units have been stationed there since 1956.

The military administration of Okinawa and the Ryukyu Islands was initially the Navy's responsibility, with assistance from the Army, but on 1 July 1946 the military government was turned over to the Army. Progressively more responsibility was given to Okinawans as the government developed. Many Okinawans, especially students and leftists, desired that Okinawa be returned to Japanese control and the withdrawal of the US armed forces, despite the fact that the armed forces furnished 70 percent of the island's income. Increasingly violent protests were experienced into the early 1970s. Okinawa was returned to Japanese sovereignty on 15 May 1972. Buckner Bay reverted to its original name of Nakagusuku Wan. US military bases would be allowed to remain and have to this day. Some of the 39 separate US military installations are shared with Japanese Self-Defense Force units.

An IJN lieutenant, commander of the 183rd Naval Attack Force Rifle Battalion, surrenders to the 7th Marines, 1st Mar. Div. on Motobu Peninsula, 3 September. Japanese Navy field uniforms were a darker green than the olive drab worn by the Army. They were further identified by the yellow anchor insignia on their field caps. (USMC)

THE BATTLEFIELD TODAY

I n 1969, the author had the opportunity to visit Okinawa on a seven-day leave from Vietnam. He found a thriving community growing across the island in modern, sprawling urbanization. There were few reminders of the war and most war memorials had yet to be dedicated. Comparing wartime photos in history books to the healed landscape was like comparing a desert to a tropical rain forest. Other than a quick bus tour where battle sites around Naha were pointed out, with nothing much of the war to see, and a lecture by a bored tour guide on the battle with the aid of a huge 3-D terrain board complete with little lights to track events, the trip was anticlimactic.

Today, however, visitors to Okinawa are treated to an array of memorials and exhibit sites. These include restored underground tunnels and headquarters. Time, progress, and prosperity have much changed Okinawa. A veteran will be hard pressed to identify any of the areas in which he fought; urban sprawl and cultivation have transformed the island. Guided tours are available and island accommodations are top quality.

Shuri Castle was reconstructed and reopened in 1992. The Cornerstone of Peace Park was opened at Mabuni on Okinawa's south end in 1995. Its walls are inscribed with almost 240,000 names of Okinawans, Americans, Japanese, Koreans, and Formosans who died on the island.

Shuri Castle, an objective for which so many attackers and defenders died, was reopened in 1992 in all its pre-war splendor. The Japanese 32nd Army Headquarters tunnel complex was located beneath the castle. The walls, roads, and paths are white limestone, the building walls are red brick, and the roof tan tiles.

ORDER OF BATTLE

US Army Forces on Okinawa

The Army began the operation with 102,250 troops, which rose to 190,301 by the end of June. Only companies and larger size Army units are listed. Attached US Marine Corps and USAAF ground units are included. Unit task organization for combat is not detailed.

TENTH ARMY (JOINT EXPEDITIONARY TROOPS – TASK FORCE 56)
    Headquarters and Headquarters Company, Tenth Army
    Headquarters and Headquarters Company, 1st Engineer
    Special Brigade (shore party control)
        51st Military Police Battalion (Companies A, B, and C) (deployed as 1st Provisional MP Bn. and redesignated 9 April 45)
    53rd Antiaircraft Artillery Brigade
        HQ and Headquarters Battery, 53rd AA Bde.
        43rd, 44th, 97th, 136th, and 137th AA Groups
        96th, 98th, 369th, 503rd, 505th, and 948th Antiaircraft Artillery Gun Battalions. (90-mm)
        834th (SP), 779th, and 870th Antiaircraft Artillery Auto Weapons Bns (40-mm/.50cal.)
        230th, 294th, 295th, and 325th Antiaircraft Artillery Battalions (Searchlight)
    20th Armored Group
        713th Tank Battalion (Armored Flamethrower)
    Tenth Army Troops
        3rd and 82nd Signal Construction Battalions, Light
        85th Signal Operation Battalion
            241st and 529th Signal Operation Companies
        318th Signal Service Battalion, Mobile
            3161st and 3373rd Signal Service Companies
        57th Signal Repair Company
        585th Signal Depot Company
        Provisional Radio Intelligence Company
    80th Medical Group
        96th and 153rd Medical Battalions, Separate
            386th, 444th, 541st, and 646th Medical Collecting Companies, Separate
            665th and 668th Medical Clearing Companies, Separate
            Provisional Medical Service Unit
        3040th Quartermaster Car Company
        163rd Liaison Squadron (USAAF)
        1st Depot Army Unit (USAAF)
        Landing Force Air Support Control Unit 2 (USMC)

XXIV CORPS (SOUTHERN LANDING FORCE) – 7,032 MEN
    Headquarters and Headquarters Company, XXIV Corps
    XXIV Corps Artillery
        Headquarters and Headquarters Battery, XXIV Corps Artillery
        419th and 420th Field Artillery Groups (Motorized)
            145th, 198th, and 225th Field Artillery Battalions (155-mm Howitzer)
            226th, 531st, and 532nd Field Artillery Battalions (155-mm Gun)
            287th (Observation) and 421st (4.5in. Rocket) Field Artillery Battalions
            749th and 750th Field Artillery Battalions (8in. Howitzer)
        144th Coast Artillery Group
            38th, 179th, and 282nd Coast Artillery Battalions (155-mm gun)
    1181st Engineer Construction Group
        47th, 1397th, and 1398th Engineer Construction Battalions
        1901st Engineer Aviation Battalion
        968th Engineer Maintenance Company
        1088th Engineer Depot Company
        1445th Engineer Searchlight Repair Company
    XXIV Corps Troops
        521st Quartermaster Group
            187th and 492nd Quartermaster Battalions, Mobile
            504th Transportation Corps Port Battalion
            244th and 247th Quartermaster Depot Supply Companies
            3008th and 3063rd Quartermaster Graves Registration Companies
            3754th Quartermaster Truck Company
            4342nd Quartermaster Service Company
        71st Medical Battalion
            384th Medical Clearing Company, Separate
            556th Medical Motorized Ambulance Company
            644th and 645th Medical Collecting Companies, Separate
            594th Quartermaster Laundry Company
        88th Chemical Mortar Battalion
        101st Signal Battalion, Separate
        519th Military Police Battalion, Army
        866th Antiaircraft Artillery Automatic Weapons Battalion (40-mm)
        Landing Force Air Support Control Unit 3 (USMC)
        Detachment, Air Warning Squadron 7 (USMC)

XXIV CORPS ORGANIZATION

XXIV Corps Infantry Divisions	7th	27th	77th	96th
Landing Date	1 April 45	9 April 45	27 April 45	1 April 45
Assault Strength	21,929	16,143	20,981	22,330
Infantry Regiment	17th	105th	305th	381st
Infantry Regiment	32nd	106th	306th	382nd
Infantry Regiment	184th	165th	307th	383rd
Division Artillery				
Field Artillery Battalion (105mm)	48th	104th	304th	361st
Field Artillery Battalion (105mm)	49th	105th	305th	362nd
Field Artillery Battalion (105mm)	57th	249th	902nd	921st
Field Artillery Battalion (155mm)	31st	106th	306th	363rd
Division Troops				
Engineer Combat Battalion	13th	102nd	302nd	321st
Medical Battalion	7th	102nd	302nd	321st
Cavalry Reconnaissance Troop	7th	27th	77th	96th
Division Special Troops				
Signal Company	7th	27th	77th	96th
Quartermaster Company	7th	27th	77th	96th
Ordnance Light Maintenance Company	707th	727th	777th	796th
Attachments				
Engineer Combat Group (shore party)	1140th	1165th	1118th	1122nd
Engineer Combat Battalion	50th	34th	132nd	170th
Engineer Combat Battalion	104th	152nd	233rd	173rd
Engineer Combat Battalion	110th	1341st	242nd	174th
Tank Battalion, Medium	711th	193rd	706th	763rd
Amphibian Tank Battalion	776th	–	708th	780th
Amphibian Tractor Battalion	536th	-	715th	728th
Amphibian Tractor Battalion	718th	-	773rd	788th
Antiaircraft Artillery Gun Battalion (90mm)	502nd	-	93rd	504th
Antiaircraft Artillery AW Battalion (40mm)	861st	-	7th	485th
Ordnance Ammunition Company	644th	61st	793rd	632nd
Ordnance Bomb Disposal Sqn. (USAAF)	204th	-	92nd	206th
Medical Field Hospital	69th	68th	36th	31st
Medical Portable Surgical Hospitals	52nd, 66th	96th, 98th	68th, 95th	51st, 67th

US Marine Corps Forces on Okinawa

The Marine Corps began the operation with 88,500 troops, of which 66,636 participated in the assault. Attached US Army, USAAF, and USN units are included. Unit task organization for combat is not depicted.

III AMPHIBIOUS CORPS (NORTHERN LANDING FORCE) – 12,422 men
Headquarters and Service Battalion, III Amphibious Corps
    1st Bomb Disposal Company
    1st Separate Topographic Company
Medical Battalion, III Amphibious Corps
Signal Battalion, III Amphibious Corps
1st Military Police Battalion (Provisional)
Company A, 51st Military Police Battalion (USA) (deployed as
    1st Provisional MP Battalion and redesignated 9 April 1945)
1st Separate Engineer Battalion
802nd Engineer Aviation Battalion (USA)
11th Motor Transport Battalion (Provisional)
Corps Evacuation Hospitals No. 2 and No. 3 (USN)
Amphibious Reconnaissance Battalion, Fleet Marine Force, Pacific
7th Service Regiment (deployed as the 7th Field Depot and
    redesignated 1 June 1945)
    Headquarters and Service Battalion, 7th Service Regiment (only
    unit formed)

1st, 3rd, and 12th Marine Ammunition Companies
5th, 18th, 19th, 20th, 37th, and 38th Marine Depot Companies
Corps Artillery, III Amphibious Corps
    Headquarters Battery, Corps Artillery, III Amphibious Corps
    2nd Provisional Field Artillery Group
        1st, 3rd, and 6th 155-mm Howitzer Battalions
        7th, 8th, and 9th 155-mm Gun Battalions
    456th Transportation Corps Amphibious Truck Company (USA)
    Marine Observation Squadron 7
1st Provisional Antiaircraft Artillery Group
    2nd, 5th, 8th, and 16th Antiaircraft Artillery Battalions
    (90-mm/40-mm)
46th, 54th, 55th, 57th, 62nd, and 63rd Replacement Drafts

III AMPHIBIOUS CORPS ORGANIZATION

III Amphibious Corps Marine Divisions	1st	2nd	6th
Landing Date	1 April 45	*	1 April 45
Assault Strength	26,274	22,195	24,356
Marine Infantry Regiments	1st, 5th, 7th	2nd, 6th, 8th	4th, 22nd, 29th
Marine Artillery Regiment	11th	10th	15th
HQ Battalion, Marine Division	1st	2nd	6th
Tank Battalion	1st	2nd	6th
Engineer Battalion	1st	2nd	6th
Pioneer Battalion	1st	2nd	6th
Service Troops			
Motor Transport Battalion	1st	2nd	6th
Service Battalion	1st	2nd	6th
Medical Battalion	1st	2nd	6th
Attachments			
Armored Amphibian Tractor Battalion	3rd (Prov)	-	1st
Amphibian Tractor Battalions	1st, 8th	2nd	4th, 9th
Naval Construction Battalion	145th	130th	58th
Marine Observation Squadron	VMO-3	-	VMO-6
Assault Signal Company	1st, 4th	2nd	6th
Marine Amphibian Truck Company	3rd	2nd	6th
Amphibious Truck Company (USA)	454th	-	814th
Chemical Mortar Company (USA)	B/88th ChemBn	-	91st
Military Police Company (USA)	B/51st MP Bn	-	C/51st MP Bn
Provisional Rocket Detachment	4th	-	5th
Marine War Dog Platoon	4th	2nd	1st
Replacement Drafts	29th, 32nd	35th, 41st	26th, 33rd

* The 2nd Mar. Div. did not land and departed on 11 April. Its 8th Marines (Reinforced); 2nd Battalion: 10th Marines, and 2nd Amphibian Tractor Battalion returned on 30 May, landed as the Expeditionary Troops Special Landing Force on 15 June, and was attached to the 1st Mar. Division.

TACTICAL AIR FORCE, TENTH ARMY

TACTICAL AIR FORCE, TENTH ARMY (TASK GROUP 99.2)

HQ Squadron, 2nd Marine Aircraft Wing

Air Defense Command (Task Unit 99.2.1)

Marine Aircraft Group 43
    HQ Squadron 43 (HQ, Air Defense Command)
    Air Warning Squadron 1, 6, 7, 8, and 11
Company B, 568th Signal Air Warning Battalion (USAAF)
927th Signal Air Warning Company (USAAF)
Detachment 1, 305th Fighter Control Squadron (USAAF)

Marine Aircraft Group 14
    HQ and Service Squadrons 14
    Marine Fighting Squadrons 212, 222, and 223

Marine Aircraft Group 22
    HQ and Service Squadrons 22
    Marine Fighting Squadrons 113, 314, and 422
    Marine Fighting Squadron (Night) 533

Marine Aircraft Group 31
    HQ and Service Squadrons 31
    Marine Fighting Squadrons 224, 311, and 441
    Marine Fighting Squadron (Night) 542

Marine Aircraft Group 33
    HQ and Service Squadrons 33
    Marine Fighting Squadrons 312, 322, and 323
    Marine Fighting Squadron (Night) 543

301st Fighter Wing (USAAF)
    HQ and HQ Squadron, 301st Fighter Wing
    318th Fighter Group
19th, 73rd, and 333rd Fighter Squadrons
548th Night Fighter Squadron
364th Air Service Group
    413th Fighter Group

1st, 21st, and 34th Fighter Squadrons
337th Air Service Group
    507th Fighter Group
463rd, 464th, and 465th Fighter Squadrons
557th Air Service Group
    342nd Station Complement Squadron
    460th Aviation Squadron (Colored)

Bomber Command (VII Bomber Command – Task Unit 99.2.2)
HQ and HQ Squadron, VII Bomber Command (USAAF)
11th Bombardment Group, Heavy
    26th, 42nd, 98th, and 431st Bombardment Squadrons, Heavy
    57th Air Service Group
41st Bombardment Group, Medium
    47th, 48th, 396th, and 820th Bombardment Squadrons, Medium
    389th Air Service Group
319th Bombardment Group, Light
    437th, 438th, 439th, and 440th Bombardment Squadrons, Light
    514th Air Service Group
494th Bombardment Group, Heavy
    864th, 865th, 866th, and 867th Bombardment Squadrons, Heavy
    13th Air Service Group
Antisubmarine Unit (Task Unit 99.2.3) Marine Torpedo-Bomber Squadrons 131 and 232
Photographic Unit (Task Unit 99.2.4) 28th Photographic Reconnaissance Squadron (USAAF)

Air Support Control Unit (Task Unit 99.2.5)
Commander, Marine Air Support Control Units, Amphibious Forces, Pacific Fleet
    Landing Force Air Support Control Units 1, 2, and 3

Imperial Japanese Army Forces on Okinawa

The ad hoc "specially established" units were attached to the 24th and 62nd Divisions, and 44th IMB, but are not included in those formations' total strengths.

32ND ARMY TROOPS

36th Signal Regiment
32nd Army Field Freight Depot
32nd Army Field Ordnance Depot
32nd Army service, medical, and construction units
66th Independent Engineer Battalion
Intelligence Unit *(Kempei tai)*

24th Division – 14,360 men

22nd, 32nd, and 89th Infantry Regiments
2nd Specially Established Brigade
5th and 6th Specially Established Regiments
24th Reconnaissance Regiment
24th Engineer Regiment
24th Transport Regiment
24th Division service units

62nd Division – 11,623 men

63rd Brigade
11th–14th, and 273rd Independent Infantry Battalions
64th Brigade
15th, 21st–23rd, and 272nd Independent Infantry Battalions
1st Specially Established Brigade
2nd–4th Specially Established Regiments
1st Especially Established Regiment
Engineer, Signal, Transport, and Service Units

44th Independent Mixed Brigade – 4,485 men

2nd Infantry Unit (less 1st Bn. on Ie Shima and 2nd Bn. on Motobu Peninsula)
15th Independent Mixed Regiment
6th Especially Established Regiment (transferred from 24th Division in late May)
Engineer Unit

Attached to 24th and 62nd Divisions, and 44th IMB:
3rd, 4th, 14th, and 17th Independent Machine Gun Battalions
3rd, 7th, and 22nd Independent Antitank Battalions (47-mm)
1st–3rd, 26th–29th Independent Battalions (infantry)
27th Tank Regiment (-) (battalion-size combined arms unit)

5th Artillery Group – 5,300 men

1st, 4th, and 5th Companies, 1st Independent Artillery Mortar Regiment (320-mm)
2nd Battalion, 1st Medium Artillery Regiment (150-mm howitzer)
3 batteries, 7th Heavy Artillery Regiment (240-mm howitzer)
23rd Medium Artillery Regiment (150-mm howitzer)
42nd Field Artillery Regiment, 24th Division (75-mm gun, 100-mm howitzer, 150-mm howitzer)
1st and 2nd Light Mortar Battalions (81-mm)
100th Independent Heavy Artillery Battalion (150-mm gun)
Artillery Unit, 44th Independent Mixed Brigade (75-mm gun)
15 IJN coast artillery companies (attached) (120-mm & 140-mm)

21st Antiaircraft Artillery Group – 3,130 men

27th Independent Antiaircraft Artillery Battalion (75-mm)
70th, 80th, and 81st Field Antiaircraft Artillery Battalions (75-mm)
103rd–105th Independent Machine Cannon Battalions (20-mm)

11th Shipping Group

23rd and 26th Shipping Engineer Regiments (less one company each)
26th, 27th, 28th (plus 1st and 3rd Companies, 29th) Sea Raiding Regiments

Okinawan Labour Unit *(Boeitai)* – 39,000 men

"Blood and Iron for the Emperor" Duty Unit *(Tekketsu Kinnotai)* (battalion-size combat unit)
502nd–504th Special Guard Engineer Units
Boeitai assigned to the IJA as augmentees: 16,600 men

Kerama Retto – 975 men

1st–3rd Sea Raiding Regiments

Ie Shima (Igawa Unit) – 3,000 men

1st Battalion, 2nd Infantry Unit
50th Specially Established Battalion
Aircraft service, construction, and engineer units

Eastern Islands (Tsugen Shima) – 250 men

1st Battery, 7th Heavy Artillery Regiment (240-mm howitzer)

FURTHER READING

Appleman, R.E., Burns, J.M., Gugeler, R.A., and Stevens, J., *The US Army In World War II, The War in the Pacific, Okinawa: The Last Battle* (Washington 1948)

Feifer, G., *Tennozan: The Battle for Okinawa and the Atomic Bomb* (New York 1992)

Fine, D.I., *Operation Iceberg: The Invasion and Conquest of Okinawa in World War II – An Oral History* (New York 1995)

Foster, S., *Okinawa 1945: Final Assault on the Empire* (New York 1994)

Garand, G.W., and Strobridge, T.R., *History of US Marine Operations In World War II, Victory and Occupation, Vol. V* (Washington 1968)

Hallas, J.H., *Killing Ground on Okinawa: The Battle for Sugar Loaf Hill* (Westport, Connecticut 1996)

Huber, T.M., "Japan's Battle for Okinawa: April to June 1945", *Leavenworth Papers* (Washington 1990)

Isely, J.A., and Crowl, P.A., *The US Marines and Amphibious Warfare: Its Theory, and its Practice in the Pacific* (Princeton, New Jersey 1951)

Leckie, R., *Okinawa: The Last Battle of World War II*, Viking (1995)

Leonard, C.J., *After the Battle No. 43, Okinawa* (London 1984)

Lorelli, J., *To Foreign Shores: US Amphibious Operations in World War II* (Annapolis 1994)

Moran, J., *US Marine Corps Uniforms and Equipment in World War II* (London 1992)

Morison, S.E., *History of United States Naval Operations in World War II, Victory in the Pacific, Vol. XIV* (Boston 1960)

Morris, M.D., *Okinawa: A Tiger by the Tail* (New York 1969)

Nichols, C.S., Jr., and Shaw, H.I., Jr., *Okinawa: Victory in the Pacific* (Washington 1955)

Rottman, Gordon L., *US Marine Corps World War II Order of Battle* (Westport, Connecticut 2001)

Rottman, Gordon L., *World War II Pacific Island Guide: A Geo-Military Study* (Westport, Connecticut 2001)

Sledge, E.B., *With the Old Breed at Peleliu and Okinawa* (Novato, California 1981)

Spur, R., *A Glorious Way to Die: The Kamikaze Mission of the Battleship* Yamato, *April 1945*, Newmarket Press (Scranton, Pennsylvania 1981)

Stanton, S., *US Army Uniforms of World War II* (Harrisburg, Pennsylvania 1991)

Winton, John, *The Forgotten Fleet: The Story of the British Pacific Fleet* (Wadhurst, United Kingdom 1991)

Wukovits, J.E., *Marines in World War II Commemorative Series, The Final Campaign: Marines in the Victory on Okinawa* (Washington 1996)

Yahara, Col. Hiromichi, *The Battle for Okinawa* (New York and Chichester 1995)

INDEX